DIGNITY & INCLUSION

Making it work for children with complex health care needs

Edited by Amanda Allard, Jeanne Carlin and Jan Delamore
With Ian Townsend

Our vision

CDC's vision is a society in which disabled children's life chances are assured, their needs met, their aspirations supported and their rights respected.

Our values

We believe that:

- disabled children and young people should enjoy the same rights and opportunities as other children

- all disabled children and young people communicate and have a right to have their views heard

- the views of disabled children, young people and their families are vital to the development of an inclusive society

- all disabled children and young people should be fully included in every aspect of society.

Published by the National Children's Bureau

National Children's Bureau, 8 Wakley Street, London EC1V 7QE
Tel: 0207 843 6000
Website: www.ncb.org.uk
Registered charity number: 258825

NCB works in partnership with Children in Scotland (www.childreninscotland.org.uk) and Children in Wales (www.childreninwales.org.uk).

ISBN: 978 1 907969 53 9

British Library Cataloguing in Publication Data
A catalogue record for this book is available from the British Library

The views expressed in this book are those of the authors and not necessarily those of the National Children's Bureau.

Typeset and printed by Fertile Creative, UK

Contents

Foreword

The special educational needs and disability (SEND) reform programme signalled by the 'Support and Aspiration' Green Paper and mapped out in the Children and Families Act 2014 underlines the government's commitment to ensuring that every child achieves the best possible educational and life outcomes and is included in effective preparation for their adult life.

The reforms are designed to ensure that all children achieve the best outcomes and we know that for some groups of children this has proved more challenging.

This practical guidance for children with complex health needs is published alongside the SEND reforms and the new guidance on managing health conditions in schools. It will help services and settings to plan for and meet the needs and aspirations of these children more effectively and thereby enable a far greater proportion to live, and benefit from opportunities, within their own communities.

It is full of practical suggestions and solutions for positively engaging and including children who have complex healthcare needs. There is also a wealth of resources such as risk assessments, moving and handling plans, and communication passports.

It is vital that services and settings have a greater understanding about the needs of this particular group of children and feel confident to meet those needs. This volume will prove a useful tool in promoting such understanding and confidence and in enabling both staff and service providers to develop activities and services which all children are able to benefit from.

Edward Timpson, MP

Parliamentary Under Secretary of State for Children & Families

1. Introduction

This publication will help all service providers to ensure that disabled children and young people with additional support needs can access services and lead a life as part of their local community. The process of ensuring that disabled children are supported in a safe and inclusive way applies to arrangements made using direct payments and other forms of personalised budgets. The information draws on examples of good practice from across the country. These examples illustrate the ways in which all agencies can work together to develop local policies and procedures to ensure that the needs of this group of children are met in a coordinated and child-centred way.

This is one of two companion publications that detail good practice in both inclusive and specialist settings across education, health, social care and leisure. The two publications form updated versions of *Including Me* (Carlin 2005) and *Dignity of Risk* (Lenehan and others 2004). The main difference between these two publications is the group of disabled children covered by each.

Making it work for children with complex health care needs focuses on children who require clinical procedures, children who require moving and handling and children who need intimate care as part of their personal support.

Making it work for children with behaviour that challenges focuses on those children who have behaviour that is challenging as a result of either a severe learning disability and/or autism.

Define the children

Dignity and Inclusion: Making it work for children with complex health care needs is concerned with children and young people from birth to 18 years of age who require additional support to meet their needs. However, there will be young people up to the age of 25 to whom this guidance applies. This includes:

- **Children with complex health needs.** These children will need long-term and continuing support, often including clinical procedures, in order to sustain life and to ensure that they maintain optimal health while accessing services and activities. Many children within this group will depend on the use of a medical device or health intervention such as gastrostomy or ventilator.

- **Children who require moving and handling.** Children with physical impairments may, at times, require help with moving and handling. Some children who have behaviour that challenges will need moving and handling – examples from this group of children will be covered in *Making it work for children with behaviour that challenges.*

- **Children who require intimate care.** Intimate care encompasses areas of personal care that most children usually carry out for themselves, but some are unable to do because of an impairment or disability. Disabled children and young people might require help with eating and drinking or other aspects of personal care such as washing, dressing and toileting. Some may also require help with changing colostomy or ileostomy bags, managing catheters or other appliances, and some may require the administration of medication rectally.

The book focuses on the needs of children with physical disabilities or impairments, profound and multiple learning disabilities (PMLD) or multiple impairments and children with complex health needs. For example:

- **Mobility** – children with physical disabilities or impairments who use wheelchairs or have restricted mobility.

- **Breathing** – children with tracheotomies who require regular airway suctioning.

- **Eating and drinking** – children who require feeding via a gastrostomy tube.

- **Continence** – children who require assistance with bladder emptying and need regular catheterisation.

- **Susceptibility to infection** – children receiving steroid therapy or children with low immunity.

This list is provided for illustrative purposes only and is not comprehensive.

Numbers of children

In a typical school-age population of 1,000 children:[1]

- there will be approximately 80 children with asthma*
- between one and two children will have type 1 diabetes**
- between three and five children will have epilepsy***
- approximately 15 children will have a peanut allergy****
- three children will have been diagnosed with a life-limiting or life-threatening illness*****.

Based on the figures provided above the inclusion of children with high support needs is likely to impact on most services. Disabled children do not fit neatly into one category or another, nor are definitions of disabilities or conditions sufficiently well defined to make it possible to provide precise details of the number of disabled children in the population who will fall within the remit of this book. However, the latest figures from the Office of Disability Issues (ODI) indicate that 9 per cent of the child population are regarded as disabled using the definition of disability in the Equality Act (2010).[2] The research information outlined below indicates the prevalence of children with more complex disabilities and health needs has increased substantially over the past 20 years and therefore the population of children using services is radically different from 10 years ago.

---

[1] The information on which these figures are based is given in full at the end of this chapter.
[2] Office for National Statistics (2009) *Life Opportunities Survey: Interim Results, 2009/2010.*

Two recent studies (Emerson and Hatton 2008a, 2008b) have given figures based on the information collected on special educational needs (SEN) of all children in maintained schools and non-maintained special schools.

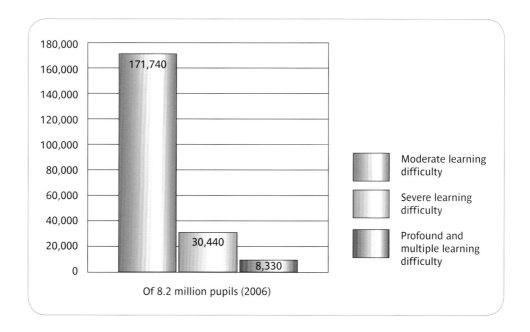

Of 8.2 million pupils (2006)

Of the 8.2 million pupils (in January 2006), 171,740 (2.1 per cent) had an identified primary SEN associated with moderate learning difficulty (MLD), 30,440 (0.4 per cent) had an identified primary SEN associated with severe learning difficulty (SLD) and 8,330 (0.1 per cent) had an identified primary SEN associated with profound and multiple learning difficulty (PMLD) (Emerson and Hatton 2008a). The researchers state that this is likely to be an underestimate and does not include pre-school age children. Using the 2008 school census (Emerson and Hatton 2008b) the estimates per 1,000 children were:

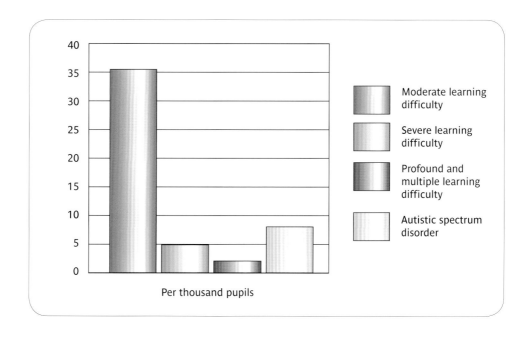

Per thousand pupils

These figures do not include children with physical disabilities nor do they specifically cover children with epilepsy. Some children with learning disabilities and the majority of those with PMLD will also have physical disabilities and many of them will have epilepsy. Epilepsy is the most common neurological condition affecting one in every 200 children and young people (Young Epilepsy 2011). However, the majority of these children will have their seizures controlled with medication. The number of children with cerebral palsy has remained the same over the past 40 years – incidence of 2-2.5 per 1,000 live births. However, the numbers of children with 'more severe forms of cerebral palsy are increasing, mainly in the group born prematurely as a result of the greater survival of these children to an age when cerebral palsy can be diagnosed' (Eunson 2012, p.361).

A recent study (Fraser and others 2012) that looked at children with life-limiting conditions (for which there is no reasonable hope of cure and from which children will die) and children with life-threatening conditions (for which curative treatments may be feasible but can fail, such as cancer) reported that in 2010 the prevalence of these groups of children in England was double the previously reported estimates. In 2007 it was estimated that 16 in 10,000 children (aged 16-19 years) were living with life-limiting or life-threatening conditions. In 2010 this figure had increased to 32 in 10,000 children. The greatest increase in age groups occurred in the 16-19 year olds, possibly suggesting that increased life span underlies the overall increase in figures.

Among the population of disabled children, there will be a number who also have complex health needs and there will be a significant group of children who have complex health needs and no additional impairments such as learning disabilities or physical disabilities. There have been increases in the number of children with more common long-term health conditions, for example diabetes. Over the past 20 years the BOX study (2007) has found that the number of children developing diabetes has doubled. This includes a rapid rise in very young children – one child in 1,000 now develops diabetes before the age of 5. Type 1 diabetes is developing at an earlier age, and the requirement to use insulin is earlier with each generation of children. This increase will impact on services and their capacity to include children requiring clinical procedures.

From recent research it is evident that the number of children with complex health needs has increased dramatically over the past 10 years. In the late 1990s a comprehensive review estimated that there were 6,000 'technology dependent' children in the UK (Glendinning and others 2001). This group of children included those who were receiving treatments such as 'mechanical ventilation, tracheostomy and oxygen therapy; enteral[3] and parenteral[4] nutrition; intravenous drug therapies; and peritoneal and haemodialysis' (p.323). This data is now significantly out of date and, although there is no later comprehensive review of this group of children, the rise in numbers is illustrated by the number of children on long-term ventilation.

Although there is no national source of information on the numbers of children receiving long-term respiratory support, nor data on the underlying medical conditions, a recent study (Wallis and others 2011) based on a single point in time

---

[3] Feeding via a tube into the gastro-intestinal tract.
[4] Receiving nutrients intravenously.

survey (30 September 2008) identified 933 children in the UK who were below the age of 17 years, medically stable and requiring a mechanical aid for breathing either invasively by tracheostomy or by non-invasive mask for all or part of the 24-hour day. This was compared to the figure of 141 children identified 10 years previously (Jardine and others 1999).

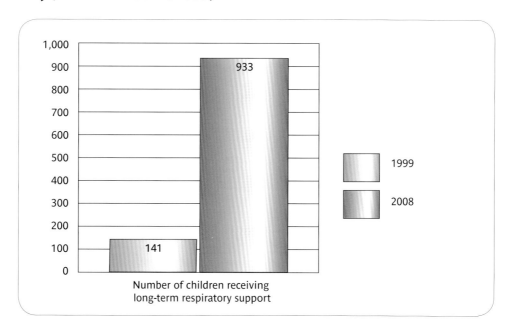

Number of children receiving long-term respiratory support

The study states that this increase is likely to be due to the wider availability of improved paediatric home ventilators and a changing ethos towards the benefits of home ventilation. The figures show a particularly dramatic rise in the number of children with neuromuscular conditions who receive home ventilator support and a proportional decrease in children having 24-hour invasive ventilation.

Definition of clinical procedures, moving and handling and intimate care

Clinical procedures

'Clinical procedures' is a term used to describe certain interventions or procedures that a child with complex health needs may require either as part of their routine, everyday care, or in a potential emergency situation in order to maintain their optimal health or sustain their life. These procedures are sometimes referred to as 'invasive clinical procedures'. Clinical procedures include the use of various medical devices or health interventions to sustain the life of the child.

Routine and regular clinical procedures may include:

- nasogastric, gastrostomy and jejunostomy[5] feeding
- oxygen administration
- catheterisation
- suctioning of airways

---

[5] Enteral feeding into the small intestine.

- nebuliser administration
- tracheostomy care
- stoma care.

Procedures required in an emergency include:

- the administration of buccal midazolam
- the administration of rectal diazepam
- the administration of adrenalin
- the reinsertion of a tracheostomy tube.

Moving and handling

Moving and handling is also referred to as manual handling, lifting and handling, or moving and transferring.

Moving and handling in relation to disabled children and young people is any task that involves physically assisting them to move from one position to another. It does not just refer to lifting. For example, if a child needs to transfer from their wheelchair into a swimming pool, there are various ways in which this could be achieved ranging from helping a child to stand and walk down the steps, to physically lifting and lowering a child into the pool. Both methods involve some moving and handling. Moving and handling is not always required – for example, some children are able to stand independently from a seated position providing that their chair is low enough to allow them to place their feet on the ground and sometimes alternative and more independent methods of movement can be identified with some lateral thinking.

Intimate care

Intimate care encompasses areas of personal care that most people usually carry out for themselves but some people are unable to do because of an impairment. Disabled children and young people might require additional help with eating and drinking or other aspects of personal care such as washing, dressing or toileting. Some may also require help changing colostomy or ileostomy bags, managing catheters or other appliances, and some may require the administration of rectal medication on occasions.

The Health and Social Care Act 2008 (Regulated Activities) Regulations 2010 Regulation 2 defines personal care as follows:

- physical assistance given to a person in connection with:

    - eating or drinking (including the administration of parenteral nutrition).
    - toileting (including in relation to the process of menstruation).
    - washing or bathing.
    - dressing.
    - oral care.
    - the care of skin, hair and nails (with the exception of nail care provided by a chiropodist or podiatrist); or

- the prompting, together with supervision, of a person, in relation to the performance of any of the activities listed above, where that person is unable to make a decision for themselves in relation to performing such an activity without such prompting and supervision.

A policy document developed by Sussex Community NHS Trust, Chailey Heritage Clinical Services and Chailey Heritage School provides the following five 'quality statements', which set out the best practice guidance for intimate care:

1. Treat every child with dignity and respect and ensure privacy.
2. Involve the child/young person in their own intimate care and be aware of and responsive to the child's reactions.
3. Encourage the child/young person to have a positive image of their own body.
4. Make sure practice in intimate care is as consistent as possible.
5. Never do something unless you know how to do it.

(Sussex Community NHS Trust, 2011 – the full practice guidance is at the end of this chapter.)

Partnership with parents and children

Services need to work with the child to encourage them to do as much as possible for themselves and make sure their voice is heard in the way their care is given (Chapter 7 covers these issues). Providing services to these groups of children also requires partnership working across a range of agencies and in particular a partnership with the child's parents, who in most cases will be the prime holders of key information. If children and young people with high support needs are to receive the very best support and a positive experience within services, there must be a two-way partnership between parents and staff. Chapter 5 gives detailed information about what services need to do and take into account in order to successfully work in partnership with parents.

Early Support is a way of working that aims to improve the delivery of services for disabled children, young people and their families. The Early Support Programme has produced a Multi Agency Planning and Improvement Tool, which is designed to inform and underpin service improvement for disabled children, young people and their families. It enables multi-agency groups, parent carers and young people to use the Early Support principles to review services, identify service development priorities, plan for improvement and track progress over time (www.ncb.org.uk/early-support).

Outline of the 10 areas to be considered

The following 10 areas form a checklist for services to use to ensure that everything is in place in order to include disabled children in a way that is safe and balances the interests of the child, their parents, other children using the services and staff working in the service. These 10 areas will form the basis of Chapters 4-13:

1. Partnership arrangements, joint policies and protocols.
2. Information on the child – working in partnership with the parents.
3. Promoting a partnership with the child.
4. Consent.
5. Risk assessments.
6. Specific care plans.
7. Training.
8. Written information.
9. Written records.
10. Review and monitoring.

This process is equally applicable to disabled children who receive their services and support through individual budgets and direct payments. Where this is the case and parents are the employers of support staff, the arrangements for risk assessments to be carried out and support staff to be trained must be as robust as those for directly provided services. When agreeing direct payments, the issues of safety need to be taken into account by the local authority before agreeing a payment and an appropriate process for ensuring training should be put in place if necessary. Lack of this process should not be a reason for refusing direct payments but individual needs would need to be met before a payment goes ahead.

Sussex Community **NHS**

NHS Trust

Intimate and Personal Care for Children and Young People

Good Practice Guidance: Intimate Care

Children and young people who require an adult to provide intimate care have physical, sensory and/or learning impairments, which influence their ability to carry out their intimate and personal care independently themselves. There is an increasing range of settings where the provision of safe and healthy intimate care needs to delivered to ensure that all children whatever their abilities can be included in activities and opportunities throughout their childhood.

What informs good practice in intimate care?

What we know from social, biological, psychological and developmental research and knowledge informs intimate and personal care practice and which promotes child health, wellbeing and safety.

The adult supporting a child or young person with intimate care needs to consider both their **attitude and actions** within the approach.

Principal elements of safe and healthy intimate and personal care:

- Trust and duty of care to safeguard the child
- A person centred approach
- Promoting the development of positive self esteem, body image and self confidence
- Promoting the development of appropriate relationships, sexuality and personal safety
- Integrating social and cultural values and beliefs
- Promoting positive lived experience and feelings of intimate care
- Promoting cleanliness and personal hygiene; preventing infection and disease
- Provision of education and training

Trust and duty of care to safeguard the child

The person designated to provide intimate and personal care to a child or young person is placed in a position of trust and has a duty through their responsibilities as a parent or as an employee to provide care which always promotes the health, wellbeing and safety of the child or young person. This includes protecting the child from abuse. Other family members are regarded as trusted adults and accordingly have a duty to safeguard the child or young person.

Child Protection

Staff need to be aware that some adults may use intimate care procedures as an opportunity to abuse children and young people. Staff need to be aware of the possibility that allegations of abuse may be disclosed. Allegations can be made by children and young people and they can be made by other concerned adults. Allegations can be made for a variety of reasons. Some of the most common are:

- Abuse has actually taken place
- Something happens to a child that reminds them of an event that happened in the past – the child is unable to recognise that the situation and the people are different
- Children can misinterpret your language or your actions because they are reminded of something else
- Some children know how powerful an allegation can be; if they are angry with you about something they can make an allegation as a way of hitting out
- An allegation can be a way of seeking attention

The following quality statements set out the best practice principles and guidance for staff and families.

Quality Statements

1. Treat every child with dignity and respect and ensure privacy.

Intimate and personal care should be provided with dignity and respect ensuring privacy, this includes care being given gently and sensitively.

Adults should take into account the child's views and feelings throughout any procedure or intervention and give careful consideration to what the child is used to and what is appropriate, given their needs and their family's culture and beliefs.

Information about a child/young person's intimate and personal care needs is both private and confidential. Information sharing relating to intimate care should be for a legitimate purpose and with the consent of the child/young person or where a child/young person lacks capacity the parent or guardian.

Privacy should be appropriate to the child's age, gender and situation. Privacy is an important issue. Children have a right to privacy and staff need to recognise that right and take steps to ensure that it is upheld. It is important to ensure that e.g. changing clothes is done in a safe and respectful manner. Identified places for changing are therefore helpful.

Privacy can be respected by allocating one adult unless there is a sound reason for having more adults present. Where this is the case the reasons should be documented. Where two people are required for manual handling, staff should consider that once the initial manual handling task is complete, the second person could remove themselves until summoned once the intervention has finished and the child has been re-clothed.

2. Involve the child/young person in their own intimate care and be aware of and responsive to the child's reactions.

The child should exercise choice as far as possible throughout. Staff should gain the child's consent or assent to carry out any procedure or intervention.

Any touch which is intended as 'help'(e.g. helping a child with toileting needs) is to be as enabling and empowering as possible and the child should be permitted to do as much by themselves as possible. Involve the child/young person as far as possible in their own intimate care and if the child or young person is able to help, give them every opportunity to do so. It is important to avoid doing things that the child or young person can do alone or with support. If a child is fully dependent on you, talk with them about what you are doing and give them choices wherever possible.

Children and young people should always be consulted about their views regarding touch and physical contact. Their understanding and acceptance of touch needs to be explicit. Staff and volunteers should check their practice by asking the child, particularly a child they have not previously cared for, e.g. 'Is it ok to do it this way?' 'Can you wash there or do this?'

Use your intuitive knowledge and experience of the child you are caring for and verbally report and document any changes in the child's behaviour or their reactions to intimate care.

3. Encourage the child/young person to have a positive image of their own body.

Providing intimate care with the right attitudinal approach with clear good practice actions provides ongoing opportunities to teach children about the value of their own bodies, develop self confidence and a positive self esteem. The approach adults take in providing intimate care to a child/young person should convey messages that their body and they are respected; a sense of value. Confident, assertive children/young people who feel their body belongs to them are less vulnerable to sexual abuse. Whilst keeping in mind the child/young person's age and understanding, routine care should be enjoyable, relaxed and fun.

Early years role modelling of good practice in intimate care experiences provides important personal safety learning for children. Understanding good touch/care behaviours throughout childhood enables the child to differentiate more easily when they experience abusive touch/care behaviours.

The gender of the adult care giver should take into account the child's age, developmental history, cultural beliefs and values and the expressed views of the child and/or parents and should be documented within the individual intimate care plan.

As a general guide children up to the age of 8 can be provided with intimate and personal care by either gender. From about 8 years of age as the child is developing their sexuality psychologically, physically and physiologically, the gender of the adult intimate care giver becomes more of an issue to the individual young person in terms of their respect for privacy, and their views and feelings are critical to deciding who should provide intimate care.

Where a young person lacks capacity to decision make the parent or guardian's views should be included within the individual intimate care plan. It is good practice for adults providing intimate care to young people (from the age of 8) to be of the same gender. In certain circumstances and it would usually be unexpected circumstances this good practice principle may need to be waived where failure to provide appropriate care would result in an omission of care.

This is best practice, however, it is recognised that within some services the gender of staff is often made up of predominantly female staff and therefore the same gender principle is often difficult to implement in practice. This needs to be explained to the child and family as part of negotiating the agreed intimate care plan and whatever is put in place should be reviewed and monitored regularly.

4. Make sure practice in intimate care is as consistent as possible

The management of all children who require support with their intimate care needs to be carefully planned. A person centred approach to providing intimate and personal care promotes both individual and consistent patterns of care. The provision of intimate and personal care always has to be considered within the context of the individual person who requires assistance to meet their intimate and personal care needs.

Children/young people who require intimate care should have an individual intimate care plan (this could be within an Individual Education or Health Plan) which sets out the child/young person's views and how they would like their care given, together with specific information to enable care givers to carry out their intimate care. These plans also include a full risk assessment to address issues such as moving and handling, personal safety of the child and the carer. Any individual issues including religious and cultural views will be recorded in these plans. Any historical concerns (such as past abuse) should be noted and taken into account.

The intimate care documentation should be agreed by the young person, parents/carers, designated staff and professionals. The intimate care plan should be reviewed annually or as the child/young person's needs change.

Line managers have a responsibility for ensuring their staff have a consistent approach. This does not mean that everyone has to do everything identically, but approaches should not differ markedly between staff.

Elements of consistency for each individual child include:

- Language – Using recognised words or other cues and agreed terminology
- Physical touch – Always washing intimate parts with a wash tool and not bare hands
- Documentation – Following the child's individual intimate care plan

Consistency of approach can be helped by checking with the child, their carers/ staff who know the child well and reading the child's individual health care plans. If something needs changing in a procedure, it is important to let all those who are involved in their care know about the changes.

5. Never do something unless you know how to do it

All staff who provide intimate care should receive training to promote good practice. No one should ever undertake a task unless they know how to do it. Just because staff or volunteers have done something with their own child, it must not be assumed that they can do it with a child or young person they are providing care for.

Certain intimate care procedures must only be carried out by appropriately trained staff. It is the line manager's responsibility to ensure their staff members are appropriately trained and receive regular updates.

School Statement of Commitment

………… School is committed to ensuring that all staff responsible for the personal and intimate care of children will undertake their duties in a professional manner at all times.

- The Governing Body will act in accordance with Section 175 of the Education Act 2002 and 'Safeguarding Children in Education' (DfES 2004) to safeguard and promote the welfare of all pupils at this school.

- The Governing Body and Headteacher will act in accordance with the supplementary DfES guidance: 'Safer Recruitment and Selection in Education Settings' (2005) and 'Dealing with Allegations of Abuse against Teachers and other Staff' (2005).

- This school takes seriously its responsibility to safeguard and promote the welfare of the children and young people in its care. Meeting a pupil's intimate care need is one aspect of safeguarding.

- The Governing Body recognises its duties and responsibilities in relation to the Disability Discrimination Act, which requires that any child with an impairment that affects his/her ability to carry out day-to-day activities must not be discriminated against.

- This Intimate Care Policy should be read in conjunction with the following (Name of school) policies:

    - Child Protection/Safeguarding Policy
    - Health and Safety Policy and Procedures
    - Policy for the Administration of Medicines
    - DCC Moving and Handling Policy
    - Special Educational Needs Policy
    - Policy on restrictive physical interventions/appropriate use of force and restraint
    - Staff code of conduct or guidance on safe working practice.

This school endorses the good practice guidance in intimate care [BHCFS/SCT] and the quality statements will be followed by all school staff.

The Quality Statements:

1. **Treat every child with dignity and respect and ensure privacy**

2. **Involve the child/young person in their own intimate care and be aware of and responsive to the child's reactions**

3. **Encourage the child/young person to have a positive image of their own body**

4. **Make sure practice in intimate care is as consistent as possible**

5. **Never do something unless you know how to do it**

The good practice guidance will be available to all children, families and staff.

Signed _____ Head teacher (etc)

Date _____

Individual Care Plan: **Intimate Care**

Name of child _____

Date of birth _____

Date plan was written _____

Was this care plan discussed with child? YES / NO

If no, please indicate reason

Agreed with parent,

Date _____ Signature _____

Please describe here the type of intimate care that requires assistance. E.g. child soils and requires assistance/supervision with cleaning themselves, disposing of soiled pad/underwear and re-clothing

Does this intimate care procedure require additional training for staff members? YES / NO

If YES, please indicate here who will provide the training and how often staff will need to have refresher training. I.e. Specialist nursing team – annually.

Who will provide the care? Please list staff members trained to provide this care.

Name	Position/job	Date of training

Communication/choice.

How is the child going to indicate who they want to assist in their care, when they need assistance and if they have any dislikes relating to their intimate care. This may need to involve the wider multi-disciplinary team (MDT) and the development of their communication system.

Where will this care be provided? Please be specific about identified area.

Detail here what equipment the child young person may need (i.e. continence pad size? Catheters, toilet seating etc) and who is responsible for providing it.

What is the child able to do for themselves? This will need to be considered in termly targets as is an area for encouraging learning and promoting independence, no matter how small the participation. Please date each entry.

Any other comments

Agreed by nursery/school etc please sign, print name and designation

Signed _____Print _____

Designation _____ Date _____

References used in this chapter

BOX study (Bart's Oxford Family Study) (2007)
http://www.bristol.ac.uk/clinicalsciencenorth/diabetes/documents/boxnews2007.html
(accessed 18 March 2013)

Emerson, E and Hatton, C (2008a) *People with Learning disabilities in England.* CeDR Research Report 2008: 1.

Emerson, E and Hatton, C (2008b) *Estimating future need for adult social care services for people with learning disabilities in England.* CeDR Research Report 2008: 6.

Eunson, P (2012) 'Aetiology and epidemiology of cerebral palsy', *Paediatrics and Child Health*, 22, 9, 361-366.

Fraser, LK and others (2012) 'Rising national prevalence of life-limiting conditions in children in England', Pediatrics, 129, 1-7.

Glendinning, C and others (2001) 'Technology-dependent children in the community: definitions, numbers and costs', *Child: Care, Health and Development,* 27, 4, 321-334.

Glinianaia, SV, Rankin, J and Colver, A (2011) 'Cerebral palsy rates by birth weight, gestation and severity in North of England, 1991-2000 singleton births' Archives of Disease in Childhood, 96, 2, 180-185.

Jardine, E and others (1999) 'Current status of long term ventilation of children in the United Kingdom: questionnaire survey', *British Medical Journal,* 318, 295-299.

Sussex Community NHS Trust, Chailey Heritage Clinical Services & Chailey Heritage School, reviewing authors Ward, T and Whittick, J (2011) *Good practice in intimate care for children and young people.*

Sussex Community NHS Trust, written by Ward, T (2011) 'Intimate and personal care for children and young people'.

Wallis, C, Paton, JY, Beaton, S (2011) 'Children on long-term ventilator support: 10 years of progress', *Archives of Disease in Childhood*, 96, 998-1002.

Young Epilepsy (2011) http://www.youngepilepsy.org.uk/

Information in text box on page 2

*One in 11 children in the UK have asthma http://www.asthma.org.uk/ (accessed 18 March 2013).

**The current estimate of prevalence of type 1 diabetes in children in the UK is one per 700-1,000. This gives a total population of 25,000 under-25s with type 1 diabetes. That means that local authorities and primary care trusts (PCTs) can expect between 100 and 150 children with diabetes to live in their area. The peak age for diagnosis is between 10 and 14 years of age. http://www.diabetes.org.uk/Documents/Reports/Diabetes_in_the_UK_2010.pdf (accessed 26 July 2012).

***In the UK, there are an estimated 60,000 children under 18 with epilepsy http://www.epilepsysociety.org.uk/ (accessed 18 March 2013).

**** Prevalence rates for food allergy have similarly increased with peanut allergy now affecting 1 in 70 children in the UK. This is reflected in a documented increase in admission rates of children with very severe (anaphylactic) reactions. http://www.bsaci.org/resources/allergy-in-children (accessed 26 April 2013).

*****Fraser, LK and others (2012) 'Rising national prevalence of life-limiting conditions in children in England', *Pediatrics*, 129, 1-7.

2. Balancing rights, benefits and risks – policy and legislation

Introduction

In recent years, the UK has become much more concerned about risk. This is, at least in part, due to a culture of litigation and compensation. At the same time, an increase in the number of disabled children with high support needs, as described in the previous chapter, has made supporting them more challenging. Many services with no experience of providing for children with significant additional needs worry that they will not be able to meet those needs without an adverse impact on other children in the setting. This means that many disabled children and young people find it difficult to access and join in a range of services across education, short breaks, play and leisure as they are considered too great a risk. Yet it is possible to include disabled children with the most complex of support needs providing services adopt a 'can do' attitude and manage risk effectively. It is also vital to consider the benefits to disabled children and their families of children being positively and appropriately included in settings and services.

Effective risk management

"Services are good at highlighting the downside of risk – but poor at thinking about the great opportunities that facing up to risk and finding positive solutions in a creative and mindful way could mean for people, their families and their communities."

(Neill and others 2008)

Effective risk management requires service providers to give equal consideration to:

*   the child's legal rights and entitlements;
*   the risks, for both the child and the staff associated with including the child; and
*   the benefits to both the child and their family of accessing a service.

This chapter looks at legislation and policy and outlines the need to find a balance between risk to the child, other children and staff on the one hand and the rights and entitlements of the child to access services on the other.

Risk

Service providers have a duty to ensure that disabled children are not exposed to unacceptable risks and they are responsible for ensuring that their staff or carers are not being reckless or negligent when they provide a service. This duty can be met by an assessment of the potential risks and by avoiding those risks that are unnecessary. If the risk is necessary as part of a child's daily care, effective controls should be put in place to reduce the risk to a level that is 'reasonably practicable'. [6]

There will of course be instances where even providers with a 'can do' attitude cannot reduce the risk to a level that is reasonably practicable. For example, when a short break service places a child requiring moving and handling with a short break foster carer, consideration needs to be given to the fact that as the child becomes older and heavier and can no longer be carried upstairs by the carer, alternative arrangements may need to be found. For many services if the child stays with the carer one weekend a month the cost of equipment and adaptations to the carer's house would be regarded as unreasonable in relation to the amount of time that a child stays. Additionally the house may be unsuitable for the appropriate equipment and adaptations. One would expect a service to explore the options creatively, taking into account that the child and carers have over time developed an important relationship. So, although an alternative placement may need to be found, it may be of great benefit to the child to continue the relationship with the carers.

Because the care needs and abilities of children vary so widely, a risk assessment needs to be carried out for each individual child or young person and for each of the services they receive, as potential hazards are likely to be different for each child in each setting. Although a checklist of potential hazards can be helpful, it can never be completely comprehensive so clear advice and guidance must be given to staff and carers on making the setting safe. Service providers must also ensure that their staff can safely carry out tasks specific to the child's needs. This is essential for the safety of the child and the carer. The Checklist for Inclusion (Chapter 13) detailed in this book provides a sound framework for assuring the safety of both.

It is equally important that the health and safety of a child's own home is risk assessed if that is where the care is to be provided. A balance obviously has to be found between imposing health and safety requirements on a family and ensuring that the care provided is safe for both the carer and the child.

Health and safety responsibilities

Anyone who takes on a caring role (whether it is as an employee, a self-employed individual or a foster carer) is subject to the common law principle of a 'duty of care', which requires that they preserve life, health and well-being. If an incident occurs whereby a child or young person is harmed or where a child or young person harms someone else while in the care of a service, then that service must

---

[6] Reasonably practicable is defined by the Health and Safety Executive (HSE) as 'an employee has satisfied his/her duty if he/she can show that any further preventative steps would be grossly disproportionate to the further benefit which would accrue from their introduction' (HSE 1992, p.8).

be able to demonstrate that the incident was not as a result of the failure of a carer or staff member to carry out the responsibilities and duties laid out in the risk assessment and care plan for that child. The service must also be able to show that the risk was assessed and managed correctly. If they cannot demonstrate that they had taken reasonable steps to avoid that incident, there are in law two charges that could be brought against them:

1. **Negligence** – where staff failed to do something it was their duty to do and a foreseeable loss happened as a result.
2. **Recklessness** – where staff knew there was a risk, but either did not manage that risk or knowingly allowed the situation to occur in spite of the risk.

In either of these two charges, staff cannot claim they were unaware of the risk. They must be able to demonstrate that they assessed all relevant areas of risk and that they took adequate steps to minimise it.

Within the area of short break services, the statutory guidance (*Short Breaks. Statutory guidance on how to safeguard and promote the welfare of disabled children using short breaks*) makes specific mention of the process services are required to go through in order to ensure that disabled children are safely included and risk is minimised (Department for Children, Schools and Families, 2010).

> 2.22 Depending on a disabled child's specific conditions it will be necessary to undertake detailed risk assessments in respect of moving and handling, behaviour management, and specific training about certain clinical procedures which the parents undertake at home. Detailed information about the child's likes, dislikes and routines can help the carers meet the child's needs effectively and help the child adapt quickly to being away from home. Short breaks will only be successful in providing a positive new experience for the child and a genuine break for the parents if the carers have all the necessary information and training to meet the child's needs fully and safely. (p.13)

Rights of access

The United Nations Conventions

The right or entitlement to access services is underpinned by two UN Conventions:

• The UN Convention on the Rights of the Child (UNCRC) (1989), which was ratified by the UK in 1991. This convention states that all children, regardless of their race, disability or gender, have the right:

  - not to be discriminated against
  - to have their best interest taken into account
  - to participate in decisions about their lives.

The UN Convention on the Rights of Persons with Disabilities (UNCRPD) (2006) was ratified by the UK in 2009. The Convention states that disabled people have the same rights as everyone else to freedom, respect, equality and dignity.

Article 7 within this Convention also recognises the rights of disabled children and young people, but crucially goes further by specifically recognising that disabled children and young people should have 'full enjoyment of all human rights and fundamental freedoms on an equal basis with other children'.

Article 19 recognises that disabled people have the right to live and participate in the community with section C stating that countries that have adopted the Convention should ensure that 'services and facilities for the general population are available on an equal basis to persons with disabilities and are responsive to their needs'. Article 30 recognises the right of disabled people to take part on an equal basis with others in cultural life.

Legislation, judgements and guidance

The right of disabled children to access services has been laid out by a number of laws, policies and judgements. Probably the two most important are:

- The East Sussex Judgement 2003
- The Equality Act 2010.

The East Sussex Judgement 2003

Prior to the East Sussex Judgement in 2003, many services were 'managing' risk by totally eliminating it, that is they were not providing services to disabled children or adults whom they considered too risky. Unfortunately, this can still be the case even today and so it is important that all service providers understand the importance and relevance of this judgement in managing the rights/risk balance.

The legal case concerned a challenge to the 'no lift' policy adopted by East Sussex, which had introduced a blanket ban on care workers manually lifting any disabled child, adult or elderly person because of the risk to care workers. The case focused on two young women, sisters living at home with their parents, where the local authority insisted that hoists be used to lift them. However, this method caused them considerable pain and their request to be lifted manually was refused, resulting in their care package breaking down and leaving their parents unsupported.

The significance of the judgement in this case is that it made 'no lift' policies illegal. The judge emphasised the need for a balanced approach to the rights of the disabled person and the rights of workers to be protected by health and safety regulations. She ruled that the imposing of a blanket ban on manual lifts represented a no risk regime or a risk elimination regime rather than one that seeks to offer independence and dignity to disabled people while minimising risk to workers. The judgement further clarifies that disabled people have the right to participate in community life, and that access to recreational activities is so important that a significant amount of manual handling might be required. It also makes clear that there may be some instances where lifting a disabled child or adult may not be 'reasonably practicable', but that decision should not be made without a thorough risk assessment which takes into account the impact on the disabled person, their wishes, their feelings and their human rights.

The Equality Act 2010

The Equality Act 2010 provides the legal framework that protects disabled children from discrimination and promotes equality of opportunity. The Equality Act replaced all the pre-existing equality law on disability, race and sex discrimination and extends protection to new groups of people who share what are called protected characteristics. The Act applies across most aspects of our national life, including the provision of services, education, transport, housing, and across the private, public and voluntary sectors.

The Equality Act replaced all earlier legislation on disability discrimination including the Disability Discrimination Act 1995, the disability sections of the Special Educational Needs and Disability Act 2001, and the Disability Discrimination Act 2005. The structure of the disability duties has changed, largely because of consolidation with duties owed to other groups of people who share protected characteristics[7], but the practical effect of the Act is broadly similar to that of earlier legislation and the definition of disability remains the same.

In the Equality Act different forms of discrimination are defined as prohibited conduct. These cover:

- treating a person (a child or an adult) less favourably than someone else because they are disabled – this is known as **direct discrimination**
- putting in place a rule or way of doing things that puts a disabled person at a disadvantage compared with someone who is not disabled, when this cannot be justified – this is known as **indirect discrimination**
- **harassment** – conduct that violates someone's dignity or which is hostile, degrading, humiliating or offensive to someone with a disability
- **victimisation** – treating someone unfavourably because they have taken (or might be taking) action under the Equality Act or are supporting somebody who is doing so.

Two forms of prohibited conduct only apply to disabled people:

- treating a disabled person unfavourably because of something arising from their disability, when this cannot be justified – this is known as **discrimination arising from disability**
- failing to take reasonable steps to avoid putting a disabled person at a substantial disadvantage – this is usually known as the **reasonable adjustments duty**. This duty is anticipatory: it requires service providers to think ahead and make adjustments so that disabled people can participate, be included and providers can avoid any disadvantage that might otherwise occur.

The reasonable adjustments duty applies slightly differently to service providers, to colleges and to schools. To avoid disadvantage, service providers and colleges are required to make reasonable adjustments in relation to three different aspects:

---

[7] Disability is one of the protected characteristics.

- to any provision, criterion or practice, that is, the way that the institution organises itself, deploys resources and the day-to-day practices that it follows, whether or not they are written down
- to make alterations to physical features
- to provide auxiliary aids and services.

The reasonable adjustments duty applies differently to schools in that schools are not required to make alterations to physical features as part of the duty. The other two elements in the reasonable adjustments duty do apply to schools, see above.

Schools are however required to publish, resource and implement an 'accessibility plan'. An accessibility plan is a plan that sets out how, over time, the school is going to:

- increase access to the curriculum for disabled pupils;
- the physical environment of the school to increase access for disabled pupils; and
- make written information more accessible to disabled pupils by providing information in a range of different ways.

The Equality Act also protects people from being discriminated against:

- because they are associated with someone who has a disability – this includes the parent of a disabled child or an adult or someone else who is caring for a disabled person
- by someone who wrongly perceives them to have a disability.

A claim of disability discrimination against a service or a college is heard in the County Court. If a parent thinks that their child may have been discriminated against in school, they can make a claim of disability discrimination to the First-tier Tribunal (SEN and Disability), which is often known by its former acronym, SENDIST. A number of cases involving disabled children requiring medication have been taken to SENDIST and schools have been found to have discriminated because they failed to make reasonable adjustments to include disabled children in the curriculum, at school and on school trips. (See the references/links at the end of this chapter for further details of these.) A positive example of reasonable adjustments made to include a child is detailed in the text box at the end of this section.

The Public Sector Equality Duty is a general duty, under the Equality Act, that applies to public bodies including public services, schools and colleges. It requires them to have due regard to the need to:

- eliminate discrimination, harassment, victimisation and other prohibited conduct
- improve equality of opportunity
- foster good relations between different groups of people: those who share a protected characteristic and those who do not.

Sitting under this general requirement is a specific duty requiring named public bodies, including local authorities, schools and institutes of further and higher education, to publish information and objectives to show how they are complying with the general duty.

The Equality Act allows service providers, schools, colleges and others to take action that may involve treating one group more favourably where this is a proportionate way to help members of that group overcome a disadvantage or participate more fully, or in order to meet needs they have that are different from the population as a whole. This is called 'positive action'.

Michael is a happy and busy nine year old, the oldest of three siblings. He loves playing football and wants to play for Manchester United. His family moved to the area last March and he has settled well in his new home and school. Michael and his brother attend the local primary school.

Michael has diplegia and walks with a Kaye frame and he has a manual wheelchair for longer distances. He wears splints on both legs to support his ankles; naturally, they carry the Man United logo.

Michael's parents were keen to see him take part in all aspects of school life and were concerned about P.E. and Games. Also they wanted him to have physiotherapy during the school day and to know whether he could go on the planned school visit that summer. They went to meet the Special Needs teacher (SENCo) and class teacher. In discussion they found that the school has an emphasis on individual development through skills and this is linked to small group games and activities. All agreed that Michael should join in as much as possible and was capable of saying if he couldn't participate. The school agreed to provide 1:1 help when needed for changing and during P.E. and Games, including swimming sessions. In class he would be helped no more or less than his peers.

The local authority were consulted and agreed to install an accessible toilet from an unused staff toilet. This was straightforward and completed during the school holiday. The advisory teacher for physical impairment was also approached and he recommended Boccia and New Age Curling as useful inclusive games. He was able to loan them for three months so that school could assess their usefulness.

Activities in P.E. allowed Michael to join in. Warm-up activities for everyone incorporated some of his physiotherapy stretches. A more formal physiotherapy session is planned twice a week and times varied so that Michael doesn't miss the same part of the curriculum each time. Physiotherapy is carried out by the class assistant following initial training with the physiotherapist. She returns to monitor progress and support the work.

A more inclusive sports day was introduced which enabled pupils to gain individual points for exceeding their personal best in a carousel of individual and small team activities. These included throwing a ball at numbered targets, standing jumps or how far you can move with one push of the wheelchair, and sitting volleyball. Options meant running and skipping could be accommodated or avoided according to preference. A few parents were unhappy with the changes but the majority appreciated a less competitive event.

continued

The Year Four visit had for many years been to a Safari Park. The coach company were asked and provided a vehicle with a platform lift. The class teacher carried out an updated risk assessment. She requested information on access for disabled visitors to the park and checked on access issues including a suitable toilet being available. The overhead jungle walk could not be reached in a wheelchair but using his wheelchair for part of the visit ensured that Michael had enough energy to climb the steps and access the walk along with the rest of his group. Michael's Mother was invited to join the visit but purely as a helpful adult to supervise a small group and not as a requirement to attend as Michael's carer.

Entitlements to services

The right or entitlement to access services is protected by a number of other pieces of legislation. The most important are:

- Chronically Sick and Disabled Persons Act 1970
- Children Act 1989
- Children Act 2004
- Childcare Act 2006
- Children and Young Persons Act 2008
- Children and Families Act 2014.

Chronically Sick and Disabled Persons Act (CSDPA) 1970

This Act applies to children as well as adults and gives an entitlement to an assessment of need. Under the Act, local authorities are required to make arrangements for a number of social care services if they are satisfied that it is necessary for them to do so in order to meet a disabled child or adult's needs. This may include practical assistance in the home, adaptations to the home and equipment, a sitting service, personal care, community based services, help with transport and holidays. The Act was referred to in the 2009 Islington judgement[8] concerning the use of eligibility criteria in disabled children's services when the judge ruled that local authorities can apply banding criteria to decide which groups of children they will consider to be eligible for services under Section 2 of the Chronically Sick and Disabled Person's Act.

Children Act 1989

The Children Act 1989 regards disabled children as 'children in need' requiring statutory services to safeguard and promote their welfare through the provision of a range of services and levels of support, appropriate to their needs. The kind of support and services provided should be designed to minimise the effects of disability and give disabled children and their families the opportunity to lead a life that is as normal as possible.

---

[8] *R (JL) v Islington LBC* (2009) (Islington judgement)
http://www.bailii.org/ew/cases/EWHC/Admin/2009/458.html

The 1989 Act, for the first time, explicitly included disabled children in legislation that applies to all children. Previously services for disabled children were generally provided under disability legislation, which did not fully recognise the particular needs and legal status of children. The 1989 Act is an inclusive piece of legislation; disabled children are part of the wider group of children in need.

In the Wandsworth judgement ([2005] EWCA Civ 302)[9] the court examined the relationship of the CSDPA and Part III of the Children Act 1989 when arranging services for disabled children. The court said 'it shall be the duty of that authority to make those arrangements in the exercise of their functions under the said Part III'. Essentially this means services should be provided for disabled children under Part III of the 1989 Act, which provides the framework for children's services. Services have to be provided with an explicit focus on the needs of the child and the family. The 1989 Act imposes a coherent framework of child-centred requirements that include, most importantly, the duties to safeguard and promote the welfare of children in need, and to find out and give due weight to the wishes and feelings of children and parents when providing services.

In all instances the decision to provide services follows an assessment of need.

> It is not, however, necessarily the case that services must be provided to meet every assessed need. Whether a children's services authority has to provide services following assessment is dependent upon the nature and extent of the need assessed and the consequences of not providing the service .... the need can be met in a variety of ways. (Broach and others 2010, p.79)

Children Act 2004

The ultimate purpose of the 2004 Children Act was to provide better protection for children of all ages. It included a duty on statutory and voluntary agencies to cooperate to promote the well-being of children. This is particularly beneficial to disabled children and young people who are more likely than other children to be known to a number of different agencies and whose inclusion in services and activities is dependent on the duty of these agencies to cooperate.

> Rashid attends a youth club run by a national voluntary organisation. The staff need to be trained in moving and handling in order for Rashid to enjoy the activities offered by the youth club. The Children Act 2004 includes the duty on statutory agencies to work together with voluntary agencies so that children like Rashid can benefit from the same services as other children. This would include support such as occupational therapy staff, from either social services or health, providing training for youth service staff.

---

[9] www.bailii.org/ew/cases/EWCA/Civ/2005/302.html

Childcare Act 2006

The Childcare Act 2006 formalised the important strategic role local authorities play in childcare provision through a set of duties. These duties require authorities to:

- work with their NHS and Jobcentre Plus partners to improve the outcomes of all children up to five years of age and reduce inequalities between them
- secure sufficient childcare for working parents, paying particular attention to the need for provision of childcare that is suitable and accessible for disabled children
- provide a parental information service
- provide information, advice and training for childcare providers.

> Sophia is a single parent. Her son, Jonah, is two and has complex health needs so requires tube feeding. Sophia would like to return to work. Under the Childcare Act 2006 the local authority, working with their health and employment partners should be able to provide Sophia with a list of affordable childcare providers who will care for Jonah and meet his health needs.

Children and Young Persons Act 2008

Under Section 25 of the Children and Young Persons Act 2008 local authorities have a duty to provide short breaks for disabled children and their families living in their area, the Short Breaks Duty. The overall purpose of the Short Breaks Duty is:

- to provide opportunities for disabled children and young people to enjoy themselves and fulfil their potential
- to enhance the abilities of parents/carers to care more effectively
- to enable families with disabled children to live an ordinary life.

The duties send a clear message that short breaks are not just for emergencies.

The legal requirements are as follows:

- Every local authority must provide breaks from caring for carers of disabled children.
- A range of short break services must be available.
- Every local authority must prepare and publish a short breaks services statement detailing the range of short breaks available and how disabled children and their families can access them.
- Every local authority must consult parent/carers in preparing the statement.

Janine is 11 years old. She has profound and multiple learning disabilities and uses a wheelchair. She has only ever been able to use overnight residential short breaks as the local authority had no other short break services that could manage her physical needs. Under the Short Breaks Duty, the local authority is required to extend the range of short break services so that Janine is offered a choice of both specialist and inclusive mainstream services. For example, Janine should have a choice of either going to a residential unit or family based carers for her overnight stays. She should be able to attend community based activities, such as youth services or sports activities.

Children and Families Act 2014

Section 3 of the Children and Families Act sets out reforms to the special educational needs system.

The Act received Royal Assent in Spring 2014 and will be implemented from September 2014 onwards.

The Children and Families Act sets out a number of reforms to the rights and entitlements of children and young people with special educational needs and disabilities:

- Statements of SEN and Learning Difficulty Assessments (for 16 to 25 year olds) will be replaced by 'education, health and care plans' (EHC plans).
- The EHC plan will extend legal protections to young people aged 16-25 while they are in further education, training or an apprenticeship. Sixteen and seventeen year olds who become NEET (not in education, employment or training) will also be covered.
- Local authorities and clinical commissioning groups must make arrangements for jointly commissioning services for children with SEN and disability in their area.
- Health commissioning bodies will have a duty to provide the health services set out in a child or young person's EHC plan.
- Local authorities must produce information on the education, health and care services it expects to be available locally (the 'local offer').
- Parents or young people with EHC plans will have the right to ask for a personal budget for their support.
- A parent or young person will be required to consider mediation before they can appeal to the SEN Tribunal. The mediator must be independent of the local authority.
- It introduces a pilot scheme to give children the right to appeal if they are unhappy with the plans for their support.

Inspection and registration

Many of the services used by disabled children will be registered with one of the inspection agencies – either Ofsted or the Care Quality Commission (CQC). Each inspection agency has a set of standards.

Ofsted uses a number of different inspection frameworks for the different services and establishments that it inspects: schools, children's centres, colleges, independent schools, local authority services, and provision registered on the Ofsted early years and childcare registers.

Social care services are inspected against the National Minimum Standards (NMS): Fostering Standards, Children's Home Standards, and Domiciliary Care Standards. Full details on the registration requirements for different short break settings are in the *Statutory Guidance on how to safeguard and promote the welfare of disabled children using short breaks* (DCSF 2010).

The exception of registration with a single agency is outlined in the Registration of healthcare at children's homes (CQC and Ofsted 2012). If a clinical procedure must be performed by a registered healthcare professional and may not be delegated to a competent layperson (in accordance with the Royal College of Nursing guidance) the service must be registered with CQC as well as Ofsted. If the task can be carried out by a competent layperson, trained and supported by a healthcare professional then the service need register solely with Ofsted.

References used in this chapter

Broach, S, Clements, L and Read, J (2010) *Disabled Children: A Legal Handbook* London: Legal Action Group.
http://www.councilfordisabledchildren.org.uk/resources/cdcs-resources/disabled-children-a-legal-handbook

Care Quality Commission and Ofsted (2012) *Registration of healthcare at children's homes* (Joint guidance of CQC and Ofsted staff and providers)
http://www.ofsted.gov.uk/resources/cqc-and-ofsted-guidance-registration-of-healthcare-childrens-homes

Convention on the Rights of Persons with Disabilities (2006)
http://www.un.org/disabilities/convention/conventionfull.shtml

Department for Children, Schools and Families (2010) *Short Breaks: Statutory guidance on how to safeguard and promote the welfare of disabled children using short breaks*
www.education.gov.uk.aboutdfe/statutory/g00222840/short-breaks-statutory-guidance

Royal College of Nursing guidelines on clinical procedures. (Updated September 2012)
www.rcn.org.uk/___data/assets/pdf_file/0013/254200/RCN_Managing_children_with_health_care_needs_delegation_of_clinical_procedures_training_accountability_and_governance_issues_2012_v2.pdf

Islington Judgement *R (JL) v Islington LBC* (2009)
www.bailii.org/ew/cases/EWHC/Admin/2009/458.html

Neill, M, Allen, J, Woodhead, N, Reid, S, Irwin, L and Sanderson, H (2008) *A Positive Approach to Risk Requires Person Centred Thinking.* www.thinklocalactpersonal.org.uk

Wandsworth Judgement ([2005] EWCA Civ 302) www.bailii.org/ew/cases/EWCA/Civ/2005/302.html

Newspaper and website reports of cases heard by SEND (Special Educational Needs and Disability Tribunal):

http://www.teachingexpertise.com/articles/excluded-six-year-old-diabetes-wins-school-apology-363
http://www.guardian.co.uk/education/2009/feb/17/diabetes-children
http://www.telegraph.co.uk/health/children_shealth/4224145/Type-1-diabetes-how-schools-are-failing-some-children.html
http://www.guardian.co.uk/education/2009/mar/24/school-trips-disability

3. History and where we are now

Having established in the previous chapter that disabled children have a right to be included in services and activities, this chapter will focus on the barriers that existed to prevent this happening and the progress that has been made to remove those barriers.

Historical barriers

During the 1990s services expressed **five main concerns** about the inclusion of disabled children with high support needs (Lenehan and others 2004).

- **Fear of liability or litigation.** Staff feared they would be blamed if something went wrong. They did not feel they were in a supportive environment where working with children with high support needs was seen as positive. This extended to fears about working with staff from other professions.

- **Lack of insurance.** Staff were not confident they would be adequately insured for the tasks they were required to undertake. Insurance companies often viewed these children as 'too risky' and the rise of a compensation culture together with the loss of Crown Immunity for NHS staff compounded worries.

- **Lack of training.** Staff in social care and education settings did not feel adequately trained to meet the needs of disabled children with high support needs, and therefore felt unable to accept them in their services.

- **Cost.** The high levels of support required by disabled children with more complex health needs was seen as 'expensive'.

- **Direction and advice.** Staff working in services were uncertain and confused about whose responsibility it was to provide care and support for children with high support needs. In an environment where finance was limited, arguments about who should bear the costs remained central to decisions about service provision. The situation was further complicated by changing definitions of health and social care as well as an overall lack of agreement on joint funding, often exacerbated by local authority and health boundary issues. There was a clear need for joint agreement on the management of risk, backed by joint protocols and joint financing.

The milestones in overcoming the barriers

Over the past 10 years progress has been made on a number of fronts and this has led to greater inclusion for disabled children requiring clinical procedures, moving and handling, and intimate care. There have been changes:

- at a legislative and policy level
- in the way we perceive the place of disabled children in our society
- in tackling some of the process and practical issues that previously had prevented inclusion.

Legislation and policy

As outlined in the previous chapter, disabled children now have a 'right' to be included in both universal and specialist services. All disabled children have the same human rights as any other children to pursue a 'fulfilling life' (Human Rights Act 1998). The right to access local services is protected by the Equality Act (2010).

Other pieces of legislation ensure that disabled children receive the support they need in order to be included – Chronically Sick and Disabled Persons Act 1970, the Children Act 1989 and the Children Act 2004.

The place of disabled children in society

Over the past 10 years we have seen a move, supported by legislation and policy, towards inclusion in every avenue of the lives of disabled children – education, health services, leisure, early years and other support services. The National Service Framework (NSF) for Children, Young People and Maternity Services (Department of Health 2004) set national standards for the first time for children's health and social care to promote high quality, child-centred services. Standard 8 focused on disabled children and young people and those with complex health needs. However, the recent Life Opportunities Survey (LOS) (DWP 2011) found that children with impairments are more likely to have experienced participation restrictions when accessing services such as education and leisure. The survey found that the most common cause of this restriction was the attitude of others.

However, there are a number of examples that illustrate a positive move towards a more inclusive society; one that highlights this is the Aiming High for Disabled Children Short Break Transformation Programme. The government made a significant amount of money available to local areas over a three-year period in order to transform short break services – services that parents had told them were the most important support to them in bringing up their disabled children. The programme specifically required local areas to look at ways in which disabled children could be included in universal provision wherever possible. The guidance stated:

> The Government believes that universal services should be the starting point when thinking strategically about how disabled children and young people can access positive experiences independently of their families. (DCSF and DH 2008, p.10)

Evaluation of the effectiveness of this showed that a mixed economy of provision had developed:

> Inclusion and ordinariness. The increased use of community settings for short breaks has led to children and families feeling more included in society. However, many short breaks in inclusive settings are still segregated in how they happen. Both this more limited inclusion and other fully inclusive opportunities were driven by what parents wanted. Some parents wanted full inclusion – others did not. (NDTi 2011, p.1)

Process and practical issues

Fragmentation of services and joint working is an area where good practice varies around the country. In 1997 Barnardo's was invited to provide oral and written evidence to the House of Commons Select Committee on Health Services for Children in the Community: Home and School. The Committee found it difficult to understand why issues around cooperation between services remained unresolved and the Hansard recording of proceedings became a key working tool in progressing multi-agency responsibility and joint working.

Despite 17 years having lapsed since this report, fragmentation and a lack of integration between services remains one of the key challenges to ensuring inclusion for disabled children with high support needs. The review of palliative care services conducted in 2007 found that although 'progress has been made in joint working in children's services as a whole, we found little evidence of this in the planning, commissioning and delivery of palliative care' (Department of Health 2007, p.13). The review recommended that the Department of Health should take the lead in providing 'a framework within which services can be planned and delivered in a joined-up way' (p.14).

A more recent report from Every Disabled Child Matters states that despite national policy at a local level, 'families talked about being caught between different agencies when funding is shared and of the need for key worker services to help them negotiate a complex system' (2011, p.4).

There are, however, areas of good practice. A number of authorities used the introduction of Children's Trusts to develop joint work arrangements (Council for Disabled Children 2006). Others have appointed Integrated Disability leads and developed protocols for the development of joint funding arrangements (example of Brighton and Hove is outlined in Chapter 4).

Insurance and liability were among the barriers highlighted above. During the 1990s advice from insurance companies was always the same: carers and staff would be covered to administer clinical procedures providing that all reasonable steps had been taken, as is the case with any risk activity. What needed to be established was what the 'reasonable steps' were.

Dignity of Risk (2004) was written in part to establish and disseminate this process of 'reasonable steps' in relation to disabled children with high support needs in social care settings. This was followed by *Including Me* (2005), which detailed a similar process in relation to education and early years settings. The process has been further developed and is outlined in this publication as the '10 Point Plan' or the 10 areas that any service needs to consider in order for disabled children to be safely included in all settings and activities.

Training is an area of practice where considerable progress has been made over the past 10 years in relation to the training of non-health support staff in clinical procedures. The Royal College of Nursing (RCN) produced a position statement on the delegation of clinical procedures that sets out the governance, training and accountability issues. This statement includes a list of permitted and prohibited tasks for non-parent carers, such as short break carers, support staff in schools and so on, and looked at issues relating to inter-agency cooperation. The lists appear on the RCN website and are regularly updated (link at end of chapter).

The production of these lists by the RCN was an important milestone in moving forward and reaching a situation where agencies were no longer having to debate on a child by child basis whether or not non-health qualified staff could be trained in carrying out certain clinical procedures.

A key component of training non-healthcare staff in healthcare or clinical skills is the nurse's authority to delegate specific healthcare tasks. The Nursing and Midwifery Council states that:

> A nurse or midwife should only delegate an aspect of care to a person who has had appropriate training and whom they deem competent to perform the task. When a nurse or midwife is delegating they must be assured that the person to whom they have delegated (the delegatee) fully understands the nature of the delegated task particularly in relation to what is expected of them. The delegatee should know their limitations and when to seek advice from the appropriate professional in the event that circumstances change.

> If these conditions have been met and an aspect of care is delegated, the delagatee becomes accountable for their actions and decisions. However, the nurse or midwife remains accountable for the overall management of the person in their care.

> Where another, such as an employer, has the authority to delegate an aspect of care, the employer becomes accountable for that delegation. However, in accordance with the code, the nurse or midwife must act without delay if they believe a colleague or anyone else may be putting someone at risk.

Applying competency-based learning and development models such as Steinaker and Bell (1979) and Moon (2002), which are used in health professional training to assess competence, to non-healthcare workers' healthcare training has been an important milestone leading to increased opportunities for disabled children with health needs to access a greater range of ordinary activities.

Because they remained accountable many health staff felt reluctant to carry out the training. Using competency-based learning models assisted health professionals with quality assurance as they enabled a clear education pathway, which includes knowledge content, practice training and capability and/or performance competence assessment. In addition, having a clear legal disclaimer that set out the responsibilities of the trainer and the person being trained and the trainee's employer helped health staff overcome their reluctance to carry out the training and organisations' reluctance in allowing their staff to be trained.

Training is described in more detail in Chapter 10.

Recognition that intimate care should be seen as part of safeguarding has led to a number of services developing specific guidelines on safeguarding and intimate care. The practice guidance, *Safeguarding Disabled Children* produced by government (DCSF 2009) states:

> Their (disabled children) dependency on parents and carers for practical assistance in daily living, including intimate personal care, increases the risk of exposure to abusive behaviour. (p.35)

Conclusion

Although many families still feel they are having to 'fight' the system in order for their children to be included in both specialist and universal services, over the past 10 years progress has been made in overcoming some of the barriers that were identified in *Dignity of Risk* (2004). However, there are children who are still considered 'too risky' for even specialist disability services. The purpose of this book is to assist services to consider in a systematic way those elements that need to be in place to ensure the inclusion of disabled children with a high level of support needs.

References used in the chapter

Council for Disabled Children, written by Wheatley, H (2006) *Pathways to Success: Good Practice Guide for Children's Services in the Development of Services for Disabled Children.*

Department for Children, Schools and Families (2008) *Aiming High for Disabled Children: Short Breaks Implementation Guidance.*

Department for Children, Schools and Families, written by Murray, M and Osbourne, C (Children's Society) (2009) *Safeguarding Disabled Children: Practice Guidance.*

Department of Health (2004) *National Service Framework for Children, Young People and Maternity Services. Core Standards.*

Department of Health (2007) (Independent review conducted by Professor Alan Craft and Sue Killen). *Palliative Care Services for Children and Young People In England.*

Department of Works and Pensions (2011) *Children. Key facts from the Life Opportunities Survey – Wave one results, 2009/11.*
http://statistics.dwp.gov.uk/asd/asd1/los/children.pdf

Every Disabled Child Matters and The Children's Trust Tadworth (2011) *Disabled Children and Health Reform: Questions, Challenges and Opportunities.*

HM Treasury and Department for Children, Schools and Families (May 2007) *Aiming High for Disabled Children: Better Support for Families.*

Lenehan, C, Morrison, J and Stanley, J (2004) *Dignity of Risk: A Practical Handbook for Professionals Working with Disabled Children and their Families.* London: Council for Disabled Children and Shared Care Network.

Moon, J (2002) *The Module and Programme Development Handbook: A Practical Guide to Linking Levels, Learning Outcomes and Assessment.* London: Kogan Page.

NDTi (2011) *Short Breaks for Disabled Children and their Families.* Insights 5.
http://www.ndti.org.uk/uploads/files/Insights_5_Short_Breaks_25_11_10.pdf

Nursing and Midwifery Council Regulation in Practice: Delegation.
http://www.nmc-uk.org/Nurses-and-midwives/Advice-by-topic/A/Advice/Delegation/

Royal College of Nursing. *Managing Children with Health Care Needs: Delegation of Clinical Procedures, Training and Accountability Issues.* (Updated September 2012)
http://www.rcn.org.uk/__data/assets/pdf_file/0013/254200/RCN_Managing_children_
with_health_care_needs_delegation_of_clinical_procedures_training_accountability_
and_governance_issues_2012_v2.pdf

Steinaker, NW and Bell, MR (1979) The Experiential Taxonomy: A New Approach to Teaching and Learning. New York: Academic Press.

4. Partnership arrangements, joint policies and protocols

Partnership arrangements at an area level

The inclusion of disabled children with high support needs cannot be achieved by any one agency or organisation working on its own. It is essential that agencies and organisations in any geographic area work together to create partnership arrangements so that all settings in an area follow the same procedures and policies to ensure the inclusion of disabled children with 'complex needs' in all mainstream and specialist services.

Although we tend to describe disabled children who need high levels of support as having 'complex needs', this description can lead to a child's needs being treated as the problem rather than the problem being seen as the barriers which they experience to getting their needs met. Therefore, it is not a child's needs that are 'complex', but rather the systems and services the child and their family have to negotiate in order to get their needs met. If agencies and organisations in an area work together, there will be greater clarity on how each service can, for example, ensure that their staff are properly trained and supported. Services should not be in the position of having to negotiate for funding to train staff each time a child with high support needs wants to access their service. All areas should have joint policies and procedures in place that outline the process in that area.

Once a local area has an agreed arrangement in place each organisation or agency needs to incorporate this arrangement into the individual policies and procedures for their own organisation or service.

Why is a partnership arrangement needed?

Wherever possible all agencies – health, social services, education and the voluntary or third sector – should come together to develop a jointly agreed policy and procedures detailing how disabled children with high support needs will be included in services.

Having a jointly agreed arrangement will:
- provide consistency of approach across an area and give status to that approach
- ensure the commitment of all agencies to providing shared governance and shared ownership of the process
- draw on the expertise and knowledge of staff in all agencies

- ensure that the roles and responsibilities of all agencies are clearly defined
- lessen confusion for parents about what tasks agencies and organisations can and cannot take on
- help to clarify the entitlement to a level of support a child with high support needs may expect
- clarify the funding arrangements for support to the child.

Who should be involved?

If possible all agencies – health, social services, education, voluntary or third sector – should come together in a 'partnership group' and be involved in drawing up the policies and procedures. It is essential to involve parents of children with high support needs or be able to link into the local Parent Forums (a list of parent forums can be found at www.nnpcf.org.uk/regions). Although the 'partnership group' may, therefore, be a large group, once the basic outline for the policy is agreed most of the work can be done in smaller task groups.

Working in smaller groups will facilitate the ad hoc involvement of other specialists – for example physiotherapists, occupational therapists, community children's nurses, psychologists and so on – thus enabling the maximum sharing of knowledge and expertise across sectors and professional groups. It is vital to involve unions and professional organisations at an early stage of the development of the policies rather than consulting them at the end of the process. For example, if your policies are to cover inclusion in school, it is essential to work with the local teaching unions and associations so that you have the backing of their members when it comes to implementation.

The policies and procedures may form part of a wider health and safety policy or include areas of care, such as the giving of medication. Each local area should develop policies and procedures that fit into the way partnership working takes place in that area.

The life of the 'partnership group' should not be limited to the development of the arrangements but should continue in order to monitor and update the arrangements.

Your partnership work should be linked to wider mainstream planning and provision. It would be beneficial to link to the local Health and Wellbeing Board partnership arrangements which may include a Children's Trust Board, in order to ensure commissioning for children, with complex health needs is seen as a priority. It is also important to consider the role of local Healthwatch and Clinical Commissioning Groups.

Monitoring and updating the policies and procedures

Once the local policies and procedures have been agreed, they should be rolled out to organisations and agencies across your area, through a variety of means – training days, presentations and other one-off events. It is important to include parents in this roll-out so that they know what they can expect. It is also essential to find ways to ensure that governing bodies and management groups are aware of the policies – for example, school governors, playgroup management committees, trustees of local charities etc.

The following is an example from Enfield's Joint Service for Disabled Children – comprising the local authority (Social Care and Education) and Enfield Community Services (part of Barnet, Enfield and Haringey Mental Health NHS Trust) – who have developed a multi-agency process to ensure that services and resources are allocated in a way that is equitable and fair.

A referral pathway and multi-agency panel to allocate resources and arrange specialist assessments where required has been established. The process was set up in 2008 with the aim of ensuring that disabled children and families could access short breaks and family support services without having a social work assessment, where there were no additional social care needs.

A referral can be made by a professional, using the 'Early Help Form'. The panel has a number of functions – to respond to referrals for children aged 0 - 5 and 6 - 17 and to consider requests for support and services over and above the minimum short break offer. The panel comprises professionals from social care, health and education.

In order to determine the right level of minimum support, additional information may be required about the child and family. This may be obtained by asking the family to complete a self-referral form, or a single agency or joint assessment may be progressed. All families meeting the eligibility criteria receive a minimum level of short breaks – the short break offer – this has been developed in partnership with parents and young people.

The panel may also allocate a key worker or lead professional or an outreach worker from the specialist Children's Centre. Where disabled children have high support needs the panel identifies the training and support that is required for them to be safely included in both specialist and universal settings.

All 'preferred' providers in Enfield are required to undertake a certain number of basic training courses. The Joint Service has developed an induction and training package that prepares staff for the challenges of working with disabled children and young people. Some of the most popular courses included 'Introduction to Autism', 'Challenging Behaviour', 'Creative and Sensory Play' and specific medical training, such as for diabetes or epilepsy. If staff require other child specific training – moving and handling or clinical procedures – this will be agreed and arranged by the multi-agency panel.

Health and Wellbeing Boards established by each local authority in April 2013 bring partners from the local authority and local health services together to plan health, social care and public health services. A Board has responsibility for carrying out the Joint Strategic Needs Assessment to inform commissioning and will produce a Joint Health and Wellbeing Strategy setting out how these needs should be met by the local authority, Clinical Commissioning Groups and the NHS Commissioning Board.[10]

In Hertfordshire a multi-agency approach to the provision of support for children with complex needs and disabilities has been developed through the establishment of a Strategic Commissioning Group for Children with Complex Care and Additional Needs. This group is one of three children's sub-groups, each of which reports directly to the local Health and Wellbeing Board. The membership of the Strategic Commissioning Group includes senior commissioners, as well as stakeholders from local health, education and social care providers and representatives of the local Parent Carer Involvement partnership. The Group is actively working to ensure that children and young people also have direct involvement and an 'active voice' in the commissioning agenda.

Using Continuing Healthcare funding

Many areas will draw on Continuing Healthcare funding to support this group of disabled children. The National Framework for Children and Young People's Continuing Care (2010) involves a multi-agency funding process led by the NHS for children with such complex needs that they need services over and beyond what universal and specialist services can provide. The NHS leads an assessment process that takes into account the views of children and families, their assessed needs, as well as social care and education assessments. A multi-agency panel then decides whether additional services are required and how the agencies can work together to fund and provide them. This process is different from adult continuing healthcare where once eligibility is established the NHS pays for and commissions packages of support. The difference is an acknowledgement of the different legislative bases in adult and children's services as well as the very different care needs of children. This can lead to difficulties at transition but both the children's continuing care framework and the adult continuing healthcare framework share the same transition process starting at 14.

---

[10] Health and Social Care Act (2014) Chapter 2, Part 5.

Brighton and Hove City Council and Clinical Commissioning Group[11] have a joint protocol on the use of continuing healthcare funding for children who have a disability or health condition that requires additional care over and above what is normally available from existing universal or specialist services. The decision on funding is based on an assessment using the National Framework and is carried out by experienced medical or nursing staff. The assessment is considered by a panel made up of commissioners, managers and clinicians. The support to a child and family may be funded in a joint arrangement, with health and social care contributing differing percentages of the funding according to the needs of the child. The diagnosis of a particular disease or condition is not in itself a determinant of eligibility. Regular reviews are built into the process to ensure that the care package continues to meet the child's changing needs.

A copy of the referral and decision making process developed by Brighton and Hove and two case studies are provided at the end of this chapter.

Adopting individual policies and procedures

The joint working arrangements in any area form the overarching umbrella under which each organisation or agency will write their own policy and procedures – appropriate to their organisation and the type of activities they run. An organisation's policy and procedures should be in line with the joint working arrangements in that area. For services that are part of national voluntary, third sector or private organisations, the policies and procedures may need to be in line with the local area arrangements as well as the policies of the national organisation. Where there are differences, these will need to be resolved in the service level agreement or contract.

The policy and procedures covering disabled children with high support needs may be a standalone document or it may be part of an overall health and safety policy or inclusion policy. The document needs to be appropriate to the size and complexity of the organisation and the type of activities that are offered.

Having an individual policy will:

- demonstrate the commitment to positively promoting the inclusion of children with high support needs
- lead to a clear understanding of the roles and responsibilities of staff or carers
- clarify for parents and children what they can expect from a service and what is expected from them.

Specialist services may have policies that set out their practices in relation to specific areas of care or support. Local policies should always incorporate the knowledge of local professionals involved in that area of work. For example, Bleasdale School, a school for children with profound and multiple learning disabilities in Lancashire, has a specific policy on eating and drinking (a copy of which is available at the end of this chapter).

---

[11] The policy was originally developed in partnership with the Primary Care Trust, however responsibility has now passed to the Clinical Commissioning Group.

What should a policy contain?

A policy should include the following information:

- The roles and responsibilities of staff and carers with regard to supporting children with high support needs. In some schools, the terms and conditions of teachers' employment do not include giving or supervising a pupil taking medicines or carrying out other clinical procedures. In this case schools need to ensure that they have sufficient numbers of support staff who are employed and appropriately trained to manage medicines and carry out other clinical tasks as part of their duties. In schools, policies should comply with the DfE statutory guidance on supporting pupils at school with medical conditions.

- Duty of care. Anyone caring for children has a common law duty of care to act like any reasonable, responsible parent and make sure that children are healthy and safe.

- What the organisation expects from the parents in terms of being kept informed and updated about their child's needs.

- The training that staff and carers can expect to receive prior to supporting a child with complex needs. Staff supporting children who require clinical procedures or moving and handling will need to be trained and supported by an appropriately qualified health professional. The policy should outline the arrangements for the training of staff. Training is dealt with as a separate issue in Chapter 10.

- Indemnity or insurance arrangements. All employers MUST take out Employers' Liability Insurance to provide cover for injury to staff or carers. Employers should make sure that their insurance arrangements provide full cover in respect of actions that could be taken by staff in the course of their employment. It is the employer's responsibility to ensure that proper procedures are in place and that staff are aware of the procedures and fully trained.

- Staff may be anxious about taking on responsibility for supporting children with complex needs because they fear something 'going wrong'. In the event of a successful claim for alleged negligence it is the local authority or employer, not the employee, who is held responsible and would meet the cost for damages, unless that member of staff has not followed their employer's policy. For example, the employer for an early years setting may be a manager or a management committee or for a voluntary organisation it will be the trustees of that organisation.

- Risk management, record keeping and protocols to be followed.

- Responses to emergency situations.

- Any additional arrangements that need to be in place for activities which take place away from the usual base or site.

In order to ensure that the policy document does not remain unread on a shelf, Coventry Council's Short Breaks Team give each support worker a copy of their Health and Safety Information Pack and the worker signs to state that they have received it. The pack covers information relating to their employment (timesheets and supervision), issuing of first aid kits, safety procedures for group activities, infection control, giving of medication, and risk assessments. The pack also contains the forms used for writing a short break plan, an outcomes plan, information on the child as well as documenting the service or activity undertaken during the break.

Intimate care and safeguarding

Carrying out clinical tasks and meeting a child's moving and handling needs will mean that staff are involved in providing personal or intimate care to that child. It is well established that disabled children are more vulnerable to abuse and one of the factors that increases this vulnerability is the fact that many disabled children need help with intimate and personal care. This is often given by a large number of different staff each day. Therefore when agencies and organisations are writing their policies and procedures they should consider the need to link their policies to existing safeguarding or child protection policy at both an area and organisational level.

Larger services may consider having a specific policy or good practice guide on intimate care. An example of such a guide is found in Chapter 1. The example provided by Sussex Community NHS Trust contains a 'Statement of Commitment' for schools which when signed commits a particular school to following the principles laid out in the good practice guide.

References used in this chapter

Department of Health (2010) *National Framework for Children and Young People's Continuing Care.*
http://www.dh.gov.uk/prod_consum_dh/groups/dh_digitalassets/@dh/@en/@ps/documents/digitalasset/dh_116469.pdf

Department for Education (2014) *Guidance on Supporting pupils at school with medical conditions. For governing bodies of maintained schools and academies in England.*

Resource examples:

Eating and drinking policy – Bleasdale School, Lancashire.

Continuing Healthcare – Case examples – Brighton and Hove Children and Families (NHS and Council)

Assessment and decision pathway. Brighton and Hove Children and Families (NHS and Council).

Bleasdale School

Eating and Drinking (including Dysphagia) Policy

Introduction

Due to the nature of the difficulties of the pupils at Bleasdale School, Eating and Drinking can be difficult and complex.

The aims of this policy are

1. to provide working guidelines of good practice for the school.

2. to state school procedure with regard to assessment, onward referrals, nutrition, aspects of gastrostomy feeding and staff training.

3. to maintain safe and positive approaches to Eating and Drinking.

The philosophy of the school is that Eating and Drinking should be pleasurable and sociable, providing an opportunity for positive interaction, and sensory experience for all pupils including those with gastrostomies.

The Development of Eating and Drinking skills will be addressed on an individual basis.

A multi-disciplinary approach is used to develop and review the policy.

All staff at Bleasdale House Community Special School have Dysphagia training as part of their induction, together with regular updates. Parents/Carers are offered this training and are fully involved in all aspects relating to their son/daughter's eating and drinking.

Staff at Bleasdale House School also receive Basic Hygiene training, updated on a regular basis.

Assessment and individual plans

The Speech and Language Therapist will liase with the previous therapist working with new pupils where appropriate.

The multi-disciplinary team will assess new pupils, taking account of previous guidelines and parental advice. Guidance will be sought from the Speech and Language Therapist as appropriate.

Up to date records of all issues relating to pupils' Eating and Drinking are maintained.

Assessment of Eating and Drinking will take into account the following:

POSITIONING
The Speech and Language Therapist will liaise directly with the Physiotherapist and Occupational Therapist in regard to advice on the seating or positioning. If queries regarding seating or positioning for feeding arise subsequent to guidelines being written, the class teacher or residential key worker are to liaise with the Speech and Language Therapist who will in turn liaise with other relevant therapists.

UTENSILS
The Speech and Language Therapist will recommend appropriate utensils for pupils who are assisted to eat. The class teacher or key worker will refer to the Occupational Therapist regarding specific queries for utensils for any other pupils.

NUTRITION
There is a multi-disciplinary approach to regular monitoring of pupils' general health and nutrition.

The Nursing Team will make onward referral to the Dietician if concerns arise.

Use of eating/drinking guidelines

All pupils at Bleasdale School have mealtime guidelines, which may include dysphagia guidelines where appropriate.

It is the staff's responsibility to familiarise themselves with these guidelines and to seek guidance for clarity.

The Speech and Language Therapist has undertaken specialist dysphagia training. It is essential that all staff follow the dysphagia guidelines.

If members of staff feel guidelines need reviewing, they should inform the pupil's teacher/key worker, who will then contact the Speech and Language Therapist.

Sharing guidelines with parents

Eating/Drinking and Dysphagia guidelines (where appropriate) will be written for pupils following assessment. A copy of the guidelines will be sent to parents/carers with a covering letter. Parents will be requested to sign the guidelines. (Two copies of the Dysphagia guidelines will be sent.)

Advice will be provided to the parent/carer at any time. If parents/carers disagree with any aspect of the guidelines the matter can be discussed with a member of the multi-disciplinary team.

School staff cannot compromise a child's safety by complying with parental wishes that do not concur with professional advice.

Requesting re-assessment

Any unusual behaviour at mealtimes should be noted and reported to the pupils' teacher or key worker, who will refer as appropriate.

Staff, parents or carers should request further assessment by the Speech and Language Therapist if any of the following are observed:

1. Severe distress of the child during mealtimes.

2. Multiple episodes of coughing and/or choking whilst eating or drinking.

3. Any colour change during or following meals.

4. Temperature spikes following meals or drinks.

5. Severe distress shortly after the meal, expressed by the child's individual means.

6. Gurgly-wet voice quality during vocalisation (sounds in the upper airway indicative of aspiration).

7. Altered breathing pattern and/or recurrent chest infections.

8. Other behaviours which cause concern, including crying, grimacing, vomiting or any other behaviour which is unusual for the child at mealtimes.

The Speech and Language Therapist will carry out an initial assessment – if there is only a minor adjustment to position, texture etc, new guidelines will be written. Otherwise the Speech and Language Therapist will consult with the multi-disciplinary team and parents.

Pathway for external assessment referral

The Speech and Language Therapist will obtain permission from parents prior to onward referral.

The Speech and Language Therapist may refer to the Paediatric Consultant directly during clinics held at school.

If the Speech and Language Therapist considers it inappropriate to delay, she will request the Consultant or GP to support an onward referral.

Consistent approach to giving oral tastes for pupils with gastrostomies

Each child is an individual with different needs and abilities and will be assessed as such.

It is essential that staff familiarise themselves with individual pupil guidelines.

A consistent approach will be maintained, after discussion by the multi-disciplinary team, with regard to methodology, placement, amount and consistency of food. Individual guidelines will be written as appropriate. These guidelines will differentiate between pupils who can have tastes in their mouth and those who have lip or tongue smears as part of their sensory oral motor work.

Definition of lip or tongue smear – a thin smear of food or liquid is placed on the lips or tongue (as per individual guidelines) so that the pupil can appreciate the experience of different flavours, which they are otherwise unable to access because of danger of aspiration. **No food should be placed directly in the mouth.**

Definition of a Taste – food placed in the mouth that can be swallowed (as per individual pupil guidelines).

Each child will have individual tasting guidelines as appropriate. The Speech and Language Therapist will review these guidelines annually or as requested.

In cases where oral feeding is contra indicated, parents may choose to accept responsibility for giving their child food at home, after being informed of the risks. However, the parents will be informed that school health staff and all disciplines working at Bleasdale school cannot act contrary to the advice of the dysphagia team or engage in action which may put the child at risk.

Staff training

New staff must not feed children until they have received induction training by the Speech and Language Therapist. New staff would be permitted to supervise children who self-feed after reading individual guidelines and receiving additional support by the class teacher or key worker.

Any concerns regarding particular pupils' needs and/or anxieties relating to the feeding of particular pupils, can be raised with the Line Manager and action will be taken as appropriate.

Policy reviewed and amended: xxxx xxxx
To be reviewed: Annually

APPENDIX 1

Staff training

The induction will include:

a)   Minimum one hour session of training on theory and main principles of feeding and dysphagia.

b)   New feeder observing an experienced feeder feeding a child.

c)   New feeder supervised feeding a child by an experienced feeder.

d)   Review of the new feeder feeding a child by the Speech and Language Therapist. (As requested)

What should be included in the basic training:

- Hygiene
- Positioning
- Reading of guidelines
- Basic oral motor development
- The normal swallow and aspiration
- The effects of abnormal muscle tone and sensitivity on feeding

Gastroesophageal reflux

• Consistency of food and liquids
• Utensils
• Communication during feeding
• Oral motor desensitisation and definition of tastes
• Action to be taken in the event of a child choking

Refresher courses will be provided for staff at least every 2 years.

Refresher courses may include

• Being fed and given a drink in different positions
• Eating different textures
• Including the child in conversations while feeding
• The reasons and importance of sticking to consistencies and guidelines
• Associated skills
• Oral motor skills
• Aspiration Gastroesophageal reflux
• Tastes – definitions
• Desensitisation

Staff who do not regularly feed must be given the opportunity to do so at least once a term.

Brighton and Hove – Two Case Studies illustrating the use of Continuing Healthcare funding

The decision to fund care packages using Continuing Healthcare will be based on the assessment as well as drawing on other sources of relevant evidence.

Case Study 1 – Molly

The following is the assessment for Molly, who has complex health needs. Following the assessment and decision by the Continuing Healthcare Panel, it was agreed that Molly's package of support would be funded 90 per cent by health. Social care funding was given to ensure that the parents could have a short break – a night out and in addition, social care also funded a nursery placement for Molly's sibling.

The assessment uses the 10 care domains outlined in the National Framework for Children and Young People's Continuing Care. The description has been shortened for the purpose of this publication. More detailed descriptions of each domain can be found at
http://www.nhs.uk/carersdirect/guide/practicalsupport/documents/national-framework-for-continuing-care-england.pdf

Care Domains

1 Challenging Behaviour
Is culturally abnormal behaviours of such intensity, frequency or duration that the physical safety of the child or young person is likely to be placed in jeopardy, or behaviour which is likely to seriously limit use of or result in the person being denied access to ordinary community facilities.

Molly has no additional needs in this area.

2 Psychological and Emotional Needs
There should be evidence of considering psychological needs and their impact on the individual's health and well-being. Use this domain to record the individual's psychological and emotional needs and how they contribute to the overall care needs, noting the underlying causes. Where the individual is unable to express their psychological/emotional needs (even with appropriate support) due to the nature of their overall needs, this should be recorded and a professional judgement made based on the overall evidence and knowledge of the individual.

Parents report that Molly does display her distress and is clearly happier when at home. However this is not considered an additional need.

3 Communication
If individuals have communication needs these should be reflected in the MDT assessment. This section relates to difficulties with expression and understanding, not with the interpretation of language.

Parents report that Molly understands a lot more than people think. They report that Molly has an awareness of familiar voices, particularly those of her parents and her sister Sarah. Molly will communicate non-verbally by smiling and lifting her hand slightly, particularly to musical sounds. Dad describes her "mouthing" as if laughing when she is happy. They also report that she has started to have "paddies" when she appears cross or does not get what she wants. Molly cannot communicate verbally due to her tracheostomy and it is very distressing for her family and her carers when she cries and is unable to make a sound. This means that individuals providing care to Molly need to know her well so they can anticipate her needs.

4 Mobility

This section considers individuals with impaired mobility. Please take other mobility issues such as wandering into account in the behaviour domain where relevant. Where mobility problems are indicated, an up-to-date Moving and Handling Risk Assessment should exist or have been undertaken as part of the assessment process and the impact and likelihood of any risk factors considered.

Molly has significant global developmental delay. She has a four limbed motor disorder which impacts on both her gross and fine motor development. As a consequence Molly is unable to lift her head and spends the majority of her life lying on her back in her cot bed, requiring constant care and stimulation. At times it is possible to sit her in her supportive CAPS 2 seating for 10 – 15 minutes a day to aid her stimulation. Her parents endeavour to stimulate Molly's development partly by using the programmes recommended by paediatric therapists. However this depends on her state of health and always has to be fitted around her care needs.

5 Nutrition – Food and Drink

Individuals at risk of malnutrition, dehydration and/or aspiration should either have an existing assessment of these needs or have had one carried out as part of the assessment process with any management and risk factors supported by a management plan.

This is probably the most complex and problematic aspect of Molly's management. She has had a recent hospital admission following a period of failure to absorb her feeds. Parents report this occurs frequently.

She currently has a gastrostomy in place through which, when she is well, she received two hourly bolus feeds of Nutrini. However at the moment all Molly can tolerate is diorylite. An attempt will be made to reintroduce milk feeds but if this is not possible consideration will be given to introducing Total Parenteral Nutrition via a Hickman line (this is already in situ). If this should happen it will increase her care needs.

Molly's feed regime is constantly changing. However at all times her gastrostomy is problematic, it requires venting on an almost hourly basis to ensure Molly remains comfortable. During feeds she needs to be closely watched for signs she is about to vomit. If this occurs the feed needs to be withdrawn. Despite this Molly does still vomit; this is not predictable.

Molly takes nothing orally and therefore requires regular mouth care to maintain her comfort and mucosal integrity.

6 Continence
Where continence problems are identified, a full continence assessment exists or has been undertaken as part of the assessment process, any underlying conditions identified, and the impact and likelihood of any risk factors evaluated.

Molly is very prone to constipation due to slow gut motility. Her Movicol is adjusted to 1 - 3 sachets daily to avoid constipation. Her abdomen easily becomes distended when she is constipated and her seizure activity increases causing acute distress for Molly. Her continence care is problematic and requires timely intervention by a skilled practitioner who is able to identify signs of constipation and adjust her medication accordingly.

7 Skin (including tissue viability)
Evidence of wounds should derive from a wound assessment chart or tissue viability assessment completed by an appropriate professional. Here, a skin condition is taken to mean any condition which affects or has the potential to affect the integrity of the skin.

Molly needs frequent changes of position to avoid pressure damage to her skin – at least every 30 minutes. An air mattress is being ordered to assist with prevention of pressure damage to her skin at vulnerable points. Molly is at high risk of skin breakdown particularly around her stoma site for her tracheostomy and her gastrostomy site. These areas are often red and discharging and vulnerable to skin breakdown. This situation is not improved by Molly's frequent sub optimal nutritional status.

8 Breathing
Molly has an unstable airway maintained by a tracheostomy. Her tracheostomy cuff needs deflating and reinflating on a daily basis. The tracheostomy tube needs to be changed every three weeks. However when Molly is unwell with an upper respiratory tract infection the tube is prone to blockage and needs to be changed on an emergency basis which requires a skilled, trained person. Throughout the day Molly requires essential suction to maintain a patent airway; the amount of suction Molly needs has decreased, mum reports they are using up to 500 catheters per week at the moment. Molly requires humidified oxygen at times to maintain her oxygen saturation levels, so a supply is available at home. She also requires the administration of nebulisers of normal saline with the addition of Ventolin if her carer feels she is wheezy. Regular chest physiotherapy is carried out to maintain optimal respiratory function which she enjoys.

9 Drug Therapies and Medication
The location of care will influence who gives the medication. In determining the level of need, it is the knowledge and skill required to manage the clinical need and the interaction of the medication in relation to the need that is the determining factor. In some situations, an individual or their carer will be managing their own medication and this can require a high level of skill. References below to medication being required to be administered by a registered nurse do not include where such administration is purely a registration or practice requirement of the care setting.

Molly has a complex medication regime which is constantly changing and at present involves giving regular medication seven times in a 24 hour period.

In addition Molly is given Movicol, Ventolin nebulisers and buccal midazolam as and when needed. This drug regime can change on a daily basis and mum reports she gives the carers a daily medication sheet so they are aware of what Molly needs.

Molly's sleep is very erratic and it is often difficult to settle her because of her pain. Both her parents and carers spend hours patting and massaging her to help her relax. Her carers need to comfort her all the time when she is awake. Molly is often very unsettled and can be awake for much of the night. She is awaiting provision of a lying board for use at night which may have an impact on her sleep pattern.

10 Seizures

Molly has a complex seizure disorder; she is having constant abnormal brain activity – a mixture of seizure activity and dystonia.

Parents describe a variety of seizure types. They report she has frequent absences. More complex and intrusive seizures involve Molly smiling and shaking. These are managed according to a seizure protocol and may involve the administration of buccal midazolam. Parents report her seizures have settled down slightly since changes in her medication and they have had to administer midazolam approximately twice in the last month.

Parental Views

Both parents are clearly devoted to caring for Molly. They acknowledge that her life expectancy is limited and wish to care for her at home for as long as possible. They are very clear that Molly is far more settled when she is at home. It is also of benefit to Molly to remain at home as she is less vulnerable to infection.

Home environment / housing

Molly lives in a three bedroomed semi detached, local authority house with her parents, her sister Sarah (aged 4 years) and her half sister Emma aged 15 years.

The dining room has been converted to Molly's bedroom. The family is awaiting adaptations to the property that will make it more suitable for Molly's needs. Whilst this is seen as a positive change by the family, it will undoubtedly be a source of considerable stress.

Summary of Assessed Levels of Need

Care Domain	P	S	H	M	L	N
Challenging Behaviour						x
Psychological Needs						x
Communication				x		
Mobility			x			
Nutrition – Food and Drink			x			
Continence			x			
Skin (including tissue viability)				x		
Breathing	x					
Drug Therapies and Medication		x				
Seizures		x				
TOTALS	1	2	3	2		2

P   – Priority
S   – Severe
H   – High
M   – Moderate
L   – Low
N   – No additional needs

Grey boxes indicate non-existent categories within the National Framework for Children and Young People's Continuing Care Decision Support Tool.

Recommendations

Clearly Molly has considerable health needs. It has already been determined that she meets the criteria for Children's Continuing Health Care according to the National Framework for Children and Young People's Continuing Care (DH, March 2010). Whilst this framework is useful in terms of eligibility it does not provide guidance in terms of amount and type of support.

Molly requires constant and skilled supervision both day and night. Without night time care one parent would be required to stay up all night which clearly would be unsustainable. In order that parents can be confident and sure of a night's sleep I would suggest that all care at night needs to be provided by a registered nurse.

During the day, when parents are readily accessible and when Molly is well, her care could be provided by a skilled, trained care assistant under the supervision of a registered nurse and the guidance of clear protocols and procedures. If this change is adopted it will need to be carefully managed to enable parents to maintain confidence in the care package.

I would also strongly support the provision of a small amount of time to enable both parents to leave the home and spend time together. In order to facilitate this consideration may need to be given to the provision of an additional carer (i.e. a registered nurse and a care assistant) depending on the views of the care provider.

Case Study 2 – Matthew

The following is the assessment for Matthew, who has epilepsy. Matthew had been in receipt of a significant package of support from social care for some time but the worsening of his epilepsy prompted a referral to continuing care. It was agreed to make a slight increase in the package and jointly (i.e. 50:50) fund the whole package.

The assessment uses the 10 care domains outlined in the National Framework for Children and Young People's Continuing Care. The description has been shortened for the purpose of this publication. More detailed descriptions of each domain can be found at http://www.nhs.uk/carersdirect/guide/practicalsupport/documents/national-framework-for-continuing-care-england.pdf

Care Domains

1 Challenging Behaviour
Is culturally abnormal behaviours of such intensity, frequency or duration that the physical safety of the child or young person is likely to be placed in jeopardy, or behaviour which is likely to seriously limit use of or result in the person being denied access to ordinary community facilities.

Matthew is unable to self regulate his behaviour. He is having very frequent seizures which are making his behaviour unpredictable. Carers will need to be vigilant and able to follow guidance within his behaviour management plan.

2 Psychological and Emotional Needs
There should be evidence of considering psychological needs and their impact on the individual's health and well-being. Use this domain to record the individual's psychological and emotional needs and how they contribute to the overall care needs, noting the underlying causes. Where the individual is unable to express their psychological/emotional needs (even with appropriate support) due to the nature of their overall needs, this should be recorded and a professional judgement made based on the overall evidence and knowledge of the individual.

Matthew goes through periods of being withdrawn and he is not interacting in school at present. Matthew has stopped smiling and laughing and currently shows no outward signs of being content.

It is difficult to say whether this is due to Matthew's anxiety, seizures or as a result of his medication. Even prior to Matthew's seizures starting he used to get very stressed when he didn't have music to listen to and wore his headphones most of the time. It is difficult to say what Matthew's awareness is of his current deterioration in health and skills and how limited his life has become but he must sense this and it must have an impact on his emotional state.

3 Communication
If individuals have communication needs these should be reflected in the MDT assessment. This section relates to difficulties with expression and understanding, not with the interpretation of language.

Matthew is unable to communicate in any verbal way. He has stopped eye pointing, using PECS and reaching for things. Carers need to be 'tuned into' Matthew at all times and pick up on subtle non verbal cues in order to anticipate his needs.

4 Mobility

This section considers individuals with impaired mobility. Please take other mobility issues such as wandering into account in the behaviour domain where relevant. Where mobility problems are indicated, an up-to-date Moving and Handling Risk Assessment should exist or have been undertaken as part of the assessment process and the impact and likelihood of any risk factors considered.

Matthew currently needs to spend most of the time in his wheelchair as he needs 2 people with him constantly to maintain his safety when out of his chair. This is due to the risk of seizures as he may fall and injure himself. His frequent seizures and current level of medication have also made him far more unsteady on his feet.

5 Nutrition – Food and Drink

Individuals at risk of malnutrition, dehydration and/or aspiration should either have an existing assessment of these needs or have had one carried out as part of the assessment process with any management and risk factors supported by a management plan.

Matthew is currently fed by naso gastric tube and is awaiting surgery to insert a gastrostomy tube. He does continue to take some diet and fluids orally but his intake has decreased. He needs 1:1 when having any oral intake due to risk of choking with seizures.

When he is in absence status – which is very frequent at the moment – he is unable to take anything orally.

Matthew finds the naso gastric tube irritating and will often pull it out. This then needs to be replaced by a qualified nurse. A contact list for nurses who can carry this out will be kept with Matthew at all times.

6 Continence

Where continence problems are identified, a full continence assessment exists or has been undertaken as part of the assessment process, any underlying conditions identified, and the impact and likelihood of any risk factors evaluated.

Matthew is doubly incontinent and uses continence supplies. He is frequently constipated and takes medication for this. This medication needs to be given to Matthew via his naso gastric tube.

7 Skin (including tissue viability)

Evidence of wounds should derive from a wound assessment chart or tissue viability assessment completed by an appropriate professional. Here, a skin condition is taken to mean any condition which affects or has the potential to affect the integrity of the skin.

No additional needs.

8 Breathing

Matthew has had episodes of breathlessness with seizures and recently has needed oxygen for this. As of last week Matthew has started having seizures which appear to be causing his tongue to swell. This has caused great concern in school and an ambulance had to be called last week and Matthew was taken to hospital.

9 Drug Therapies and Medication

The location of care will influence who gives the medication. In determining the level of need, it is the knowledge and skill required to manage the clinical need and the interaction of the medication in relation to the need that is the determining factor. In some situations, an individual or their carer will be managing their own medication and this can require a high level of skill. References below to medication being required to be administered by a registered nurse do not include where such administration is purely a registration or practice requirement of the care setting.

Matthew has drug resistant epilepsy. He is on 4 different medications for his epilepsy and 10 different medications in total.

Paediatrician input is currently required at least weekly in order to achieve appropriate drug levels.

Matthew also has an emergency medication protocol which involves the administration of buccal midazolam, then calling an ambulance and the administration of Rectal Paraldehyde. He is currently needing buccal midazolam at least weekly.

10 Seizures

Matthew is currently, frequently having almost continuous seizure activity. This consists of

- *atypical absence seizures which are commonly resulting in status epilepticus*
- *tonic seizures – as previously discussed, now resulting in tongue swelling and possible compromised breathing*
- *drop seizures – this means he requires 1:1 at all times and has to wear a specially modified helmet because of the frequent injuries these seizures were causing.*

A recent 24 hour EEG monitoring confirmed that Matthew was having almost continuous seizures and up to x7 tonic seizures a night.

His seizures have deteriorated so severely recently that he is now unable to take an adequate oral intake and has had a naso gastric tube passed.

Parental Views

Both parents were present at the assessment and have read the completed assessment. They agree with all the assessment and the assessed domain levels.

Assessed Levels of Need

Care Domain	P	S	H	M	L	N
Challenging Behaviour				x		
Psychological Needs				x		
Communication			x			
Mobility			x			
Nutrition – Food and Drink				x		
Continence				x		
Skin (including tissue viability)						x
Breathing				x		
Drug Therapies and Medication			x			
Seizures		x				
TOTALS		1	3	5		1

P   – Priority
S   – Severe
H   – High
M   – Moderate
L   – Low
N   – No additional needs

Grey boxes indicate non-existent categories within the National Framework for Children and Young People's Continuing Care Decision Support Tool.

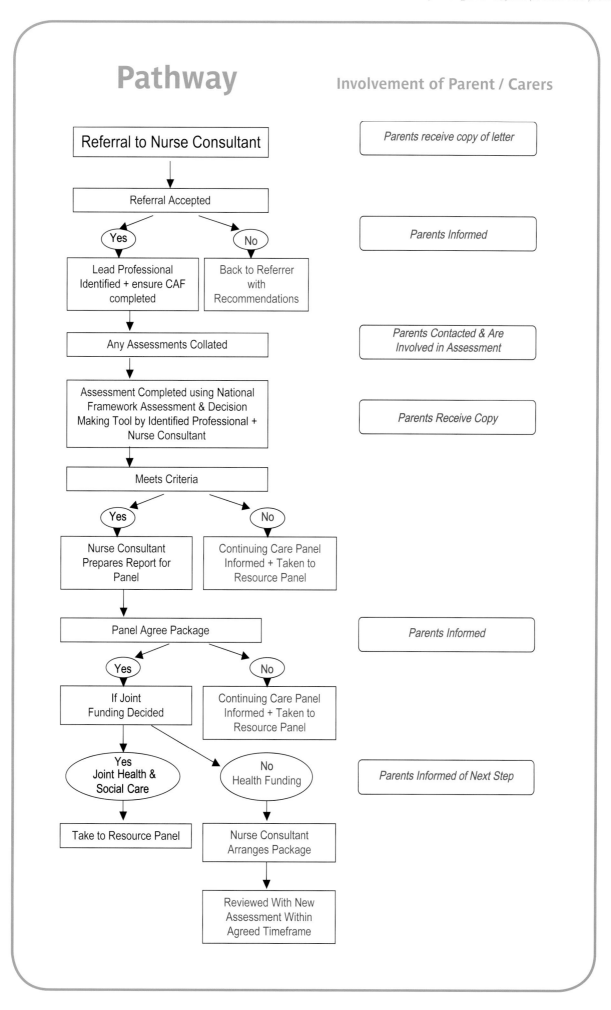

Pathway   Involvement of Parent / Carers

Referral to Nurse Consultant — *Parents receive copy of letter*

Referral Accepted

Yes → Lead Professional Identified + ensure CAF completed

No → Back to Referrer with Recommendations — *Parents Informed*

Any Assessments Collated — *Parents Contacted & Are Involved in Assessment*

Assessment Completed using National Framework Assessment & Decision Making Tool by Identified Professional + Nurse Consultant — *Parents Receive Copy*

Meets Criteria

Yes → Nurse Consultant Prepares Report for Panel

No → Continuing Care Panel Informed + Taken to Resource Panel

Panel Agree Package — *Parents Informed*

Yes → If Joint Funding Decided

No → Continuing Care Panel Informed + Taken to Resource Panel

Yes Joint Health & Social Care

No Health Funding — *Parents Informed of Next Step*

Take to Resource Panel

Nurse Consultant Arranges Package

Reviewed With New Assessment Within Agreed Timeframe

5. Information on the child – working in partnership with parents

The organisation offering a service to a child will need to hold information about that child, including details about the child's disability, medical condition and support needs. This information is required in order to plan a service or activity so that it is inclusive and minimises the risks to the child and staff.

Obtaining information

Parents usually have prime responsibility for their children and therefore hold the information about their child. They should inform the organisation or service about their child's disability, medical condition and additional support needs. However, there is no requirement on them to do so, and parents may decide not to tell a service about a particular condition. Many parents have found that if they tell a service about all their child's needs the service will respond by stating that their child is 'too disabled' to attend. Therefore, if the service is committed to inclusion it will need to take a proactive role: asking parents about their child's needs, promoting an atmosphere that is open and in which parents feel comfortable to disclose information, safe in the knowledge that such information:

- will be communicated to staff who need to know that information
- will be used sensitively to help their child make the most of their time
- will not be used to bar their child from the service or from specific activities.

Parents employing support staff or personal assistants using direct payments and other forms of personalised budgets need to ensure that those staff have all the information they need in order to support the child in a safe and inclusive way.

Services may use forms such as 'All About Me' profiles or booklets to gather this information in a child-centred way. An example of an 'All About Me' profile developed by the Family Placement Services in Cornwall can be found at the end of this chapter. Parents may prepare this type of information before their child enters a service. Another resource that may be of help to parents when sharing information about their child and family has been developed by the Early Support programme and can be downloaded from:
www.councilfordisabledchildren.org.uk/what-we-do/networks-campaigns/early-support

Increasingly, use is being made of smartphone and web-based apps to support communication and information sharing. Early Support have developed an app that is a smartphone and web-based interactive version of the Family Held Record mentioned above.

Some of the medical information that is required by a service will need to be verified by a medical practitioner. For example, if a service is required to administer medication, the dosages will need to be verified by the child's GP or paediatrician.

If the service is a mainstream or universal service, the general admission form should contain a question that will pick up that the child has additional support needs. In these services, often an additional form will be provided for the children who need it.

All information on a child will need to be regularly updated as the child's needs change and develop. The review process in education and social services can be a useful time to ensure that information on the child is up to date.

Information sharing and confidentiality

One of the dilemmas facing any service is how much of the information about the child should be shared and with whom and how much should remain confidential and private. The service needs to weigh up the rights and risks, taking into account the views of the parents and in some instances those of the child and make a decision for each individual child. The decision will often depend on the particular condition of the child, or the age and level of understanding of the child. For example, if a child is allergic to certain foods and likely to go into anaphylactic shock, the information about the child's allergies will need to be shared with both staff and other children. On the other hand, if a teenager has a bowel condition, he might not want that information shared with staff who did not need to know or with the other young people.

The child's safety will always be the first consideration.

The legislation recognises that a request for confidentiality may limit the reasonable adjustments that a school can make. Disabled pupils and their parents have a right to request that a pupil's disability be treated as confidential. In which case what is reasonable for the school to do must be consistent with the request for confidentiality. The school still has a duty to make reasonable adjustments but might make different adjustments from those it would have made if there had not been a confidentiality request.

If a request for confidentiality meant that staff taking pupils on a trip could not be informed of the nature of a child's condition, and if ignorance of the child's condition could put the child at risk, the school might not be able to include the pupil on that trip. Although they would first need to consider whether an alternative trip, the provision of additional assistance or allowing the disabled pupil to attend for only some of the trip might mitigate the risk and enable the disabled pupil to attend.

In practice, the very reasons that parents may request confidentiality relate back to concerns that information might not be used sensitively to support their child, or that their child might be singled out in some way. Parents' concerns are likely to be heightened where there is a social stigma attached to the child's health condition.

It comes back to the same principle as above: if parents are confident that information they share with the school will be handled sensitively, parents are more likely to share it in the first place and less likely to request confidentiality if they do share it.

Passing on information

With the consent of the parents and/or young people, information should be shared and passed on from one service to another, particularly at stages of transition. For example, in order to ensure the smooth transfer from one school to the next, schools should be informed about additional support needs, well in advance. To meet high support needs, schools may require time to plan and to make reasonable adjustments or to put into place support arrangements. The example from Derbyshire illustrates the planning and sharing of information during the transition to school.

Anna is a little girl with profound and complex needs who has received a service to enable parents to return to work. The Disability Inclusion Service in Derbyshire supported her in a private nursery and then into a mainstream school, where she also attends the breakfast and after school club.

Anna has a diagnosis of Periventricular Leukomalacia with Microcephaly, global developmental delay, developmental dysplasia of the hip, corticovisual impairment and is under investigation for a food intolerance/ reflux. Anna receives support from a large multi-agency team, which includes physiotherapy, speech and language therapy, occupational therapy as well as support from the Service for Visual Impairment and the Disability Inclusion Service.

Anna started attending a day nursery when she was five months old. When she was two years old additional funding was provided by the Disability Inclusion Service to cover the extra support that Anna needed in order to be included in the nursery. Funding was also made available to provide additional storage for Anna's equipment, and pay for staffing cover whilst nursery staff attended moving and handling training.

When Anna reached school age her mother and pre-school support teacher were keen to ensure that a plan was in place enabling a smooth and positive transition into school. The Inclusion Officer and an SEN teaching assistant linked with them and the other members of the Team Around the Child to ensure that the necessary support would be in place so that Anna could be successfully included in a mainstream school. An initial meeting took place in April to identify the support that would be required in preparation for the start of the school term in September. It was also agreed at a statutory assessment review that Anna would need to access the school's breakfast and after school club. Anna's SEN statement agreed that she would receive 25 hours per week support in the classroom.

An additional 10 hours of staffing support was given to aid the planning stage during Anna's transition to school. This provided time for staff to prepare resources, to support Anna during her visits and to complete the necessary plans – a care plan, healthcare plan, moving and handling plan, and a personal emergency evacuation plan as well as the risk assessments. It was agreed that each plan could be used by school and the breakfast and after school clubs as all are on the same premises. The SEN teaching assistant visited the nursery and met Anna and her pre-school support teacher. This provided a good opportunity for her to gain information from key members of staff at nursery – for example they discussed Anna's sensory needs, her communication style, and the types of activities she enjoyed. The pre-school support teacher completed a personal passport to support her transition.

Initially additional staffing support was provided for six hours per week in the first term, from September to December (funding was extended after the first term). At a meeting it was decided that due to Anna attending breakfast and after school club on the school premises, there needed to be a clear distinction between the structure of school and the more social environment of the after school club. The SEN teaching assistant suggested that this could be facilitated by the additional staff member providing an opportunity for Anna to relax, and play in the sensory room at the end of school. Her personal care needs would then be met before she joined her friends in the after school club. Anna's parents moved her equipment from the nursery to the school. Staff at the after school club altered the layout of the room to ensure that Anna could access all areas and her independence could be encouraged. A café style snack was introduced that promoted the independence skill of all the children and also freed up a member of staff at snack time to support Anna.

Staff at the after school club have worked in a way that kept support at a safe but minimal level to ensure that Anna had the space to develop independence and friendships with her peers. Developing her own friendships has meant that her sister, who also attended, did not take on the role of her carer. To ensure good communication between the various settings each day a communication book was introduced.

It is also important to remember that parents of disabled children often find themselves having to give the same information again and again to the many different sets of professionals involved in their child's life. If a child has a passport or profile it is important that it is not simply filed away but used by different services to complete their own forms and parents are only asked for information that is missing from the profile or passport.

As part of its multi-agency service for disabled children Enfield Council has developed an Early Intervention Support Service (EISS), which works to ensure that information on the child is passed on to schools and nurseries in a timely and effective manner. It also offers support to young children entering nursery or school for the first time through a team of Specialist Teaching Assistants (STAs) who work in the Foundation Stage Support Team. (A full description of this service is at the end of this chapter.)

Providing information to staff

Larger organisations or agencies, for example local authorities, may produce general information on particular conditions. It is important that this information gives staff an understanding about a particular condition as well as how it is likely to affect the child in their setting. This type of information should not be seen to replace staff training or information about an individual child's particular needs provided by a health professional. Organisations providing specialist services to specific groups of children may also give information to their staff on specific conditions – for example, a service providing horse riding to disabled children with epilepsy may have information leaflets on epilepsy and how it may affect the children in relation to horse riding.

However, general information can be found on various websites. Parents may suggest websites they have found helpful in understanding their child's condition and how it impacts on their life. Most national organisations supporting individuals with a specific condition have websites containing general information on that condition. For example, the Brittle Bone Society (www.brittlebone.org) produces an information sheet for schools and early years settings on the condition as well as practical general guidelines on seating, moving about in school, outside play supervision and so on. This information can be used and adapted by other services and activities. Once again, this general information does not replace information about an individual child's specific needs, which should be provided by a health professional who knows the child well.

It may also be helpful for staff to understand that there may be some issues such as poor sleep that are more likely to be experienced by disabled children, and impact on their ability to learn or enjoy activities. There is a section on sleep in the resources section of this chapter.

Staff may want to know more about the medicines a child uses. The Medicines for Children website (www.medicinesforchildren.org.uk) provides information that is easy to read and is written mainly for parents so can be understood by non-health qualified staff.

Contact a Family (www.cafamily.org.uk) is a national organisation that operates an advice helpline and produces useful resources, including a comprehensive directory of rare conditions (www.cafamily.org.uk/medical-information/conditions/). This directory also offers links to organisations that offer support around a particular condition many of which produce materials and resources that can be helpful to parents and services.

Parents may prepare information about their child, explaining their condition and how this impacts on the child. The following examples illustrate the increasing use of profiles, written in a child-centred, easy to understand format.

> ## NIFTY (Neurofibromatosis Information File Tailored For You) © MMU 2012
>
> *Carly Jim[12] is a parent of a young child with a genetic condition, Neurofibromatosis type 1 (NF1). Carly has worked with other parents and adults with NF1, the Manchester Neurofibromatosis clinic team, The Neuro Foundation and Children with Tumours to develop a resource that can be used to share information with services about an individual child and the condition. The file was developed because there is great variability in NF1, both between different children with the illness and in the life course of an individual child. This meant that current methods for information sharing (such as general information sheets) are insufficient to convey the specific impact that having NF1 has on that child's life.*
>
> *NIFTY © MMU 2012 contains medical information specific to the child as well as personal information (child's likes and dislikes) and practical advice relating to the support needed. The aim of NIFTY is to enable someone with no prior knowledge of NF to support the child's safe inclusion in social, educational and community activities. It is not intended as an exhaustive resource and is not a substitute for getting medical advice. A number of key pages of NIFTY are shown below. Please note, this file is still in development, for further information please contact Dr Carly Jim at c.jim@mmu.ac.uk.*

Resource examples:

1. All About Me – Developed by the Family Placement Service in consultation with the Residential Short Break Providers, Cornwall Council.

2. Case study – Early Intervention Support Service, Enfield Council.

3. Sleep – Information and resources.

4. NF1 file – (Only selected pages to be reproduced).

---

[12] In her professional capacity Dr Carly Jim is a chartered health psychologist and a post doctoral researcher in the Research Institute for Health and Social Change at Manchester Metropolitan University. She is working with Professor Juliet Goldbart to develop and pilot the use of the NIFTY© MMU 2012.

Family Based Short Break Care

PLACEMENT AGREEMENT MEETING – PART A

ALL ABOUT ME

WHERE I LIVE AND WHO I LIVE WITH:

My name and what I like to be called

Address of person/s I live with (parental responsibility)

Telephone number:

Name of person/s I live with (parental responsibility)

My date of birth

MY NHS Number:

My social worker:

People who are important to me:

Pets who live with me:

Friends I like to play with:

Things I like to play with:

WHO ELSE SUPPORTS ME?

Name of my Family Based Carer and their Tel No:

Name, Address & Tel No of my GP:

Name, Address & Tel No of my dentist:

Name and contact details of any other professionals involved in my care and looking after me:

Name and contact details of any other people involved in my care or social activities:

HEALTH:

You need to know this about my health:

I take this medication: and this is how and when I take it:
(Parent – please tell us how you administer your child's medication.)

Allergies: (Please tell us if you are allergic to anything.)

Parent – please tell us if your child has epilepsy and has a current Epilepsy Profile with Support Plan. Please give a copy of the Profile and Plan to the Short Break Carer: (Placement cannot commence until this has been provided.)

COMMUNICATION:

This is how I communicate:

Do you have a communication passport at school? If so can a copy be provided to the carers?

This is the name of my speech and language therapist:

USING THE TOILET:

To promote my independence and respect my dignity, please offer me the following support:

EATING AND FOOD CHOICES:

This is what I like to eat and more importantly what I don't like to eat:

Do you need special cutlery, plates etc. or have a special diet or like your food served in a special way?

WASHING & DRESSING:

This is how I wash and get dressed: (Please tell us if you prefer a bath or shower and if you like help in choosing your own clothes and getting dressed.)

GETTING ABOUT:

This is how I get about: (Please tell us if you require assistance with your mobility and if you are used to travelling on buses, in cars and on trains.)

SLEEPING:

This is my bedtime routine (including any comforters) and how you can help me to sleep well:

Do you need assistance at night with toileting (are nappies/pads used)?

Do you need to rest during the day, if so how long and where?

SAFETY:
This is how to keep me safe:

Do you need to be kept safe when near animals/pets?

EMERGENCY HELP:

Please contact these people in event of an emergency:

FAITH AND CULTURAL IDENTITY:

Please tell us if you have a practising faith and if we should observe any religious customs or cultural practices that are important to you.

EDUCATION:

Where do you go to school?

What time do you go to and leave school?

Who is your teacher?

ADDITIONAL INFORMATION:
Other things are important to your child?

Parent – please tell us anything you think may be important to help us understand your child and make their stay a happy one.

Parent – please advise the carer(s) of any known risks not already identified:

Parent – please tell us if your child has known behaviours which require specific intervention.

Enfield Council

Early Intervention Support Service (EISS)

Early Intervention Support Service (EISS) represents education within the Joint Service for Disabled Children and provides:

- A home visiting teaching service – the Pre-School Support Team
- A keyworking service for families of children with complex needs – Early Support
- Support for young children with special needs and disabilities in their transition into school – the Foundation Stage Support Team.

The initial referral

In Enfield, children between the age of birth to three who are identified as having special needs or disabilities are referred to the Early Intervention Support Service from a variety of sources, for example paediatricians, health visitors, speech and language therapists and physiotherapists. Parents can also self-refer. Children referred may be allocated a home visiting teacher and/ or a keyworker from Early Support, dependent on individual needs at that time. Therefore a high proportion of children with special needs in Enfield are known to EISS from a young age, and their families are supported by the team in making the arrangements required for transition into a school nursery at the age of three.

Enfield operates a priority system for placing children with special needs, disabilities and medical needs in mainstream nurseries. The system is administered by the local authority Special Educational Needs Services (SEN Services) and aims to ensure that all children identified with SEN are given an early opportunity to access education.

In February of each year, all professionals in Enfield inform SEN Services (with parental permission) of any children they know who would benefit from a priority placement. Children who meet the criteria are offered a place in an Enfield mainstream school nursery closest to their home. Parents are also able to make their own application to the school of their choice, and if successful, are free to choose which one best meets the needs of the child and the family.

Once a nursery place has been accepted, the home visiting teachers will work in partnership with the parent to liaise with the school, to ensure a smooth transition is effected for all involved. Schools receive transition reports from Children's Centres, and private, voluntary and independent settings if they have children starting who are in daycare placements. Settings are kept informed of their duty to provide this information through their meetings with local authority representatives and schools also have a responsibility to actively seek this information from the settings in good time.

During the latter part of the summer term, the home visiting teachers work with the parents in their own home to prepare a Transition Passport; a simple, child-centred document that speaks from the child's perspective. Within the passport, with the help of photographs, the child introduces themselves and their family, and tells the reader all about themselves; important people in their lives, their likes, dislikes, how they communicate, their favourite activities, what they might need help with, what might frighten them and what makes them feel happy. At the back of this document in a separate section, all professional reports are also included, but the focus of the passport is the child's voice. This process also enables the parent to share information that may not have been discussed, such as how to settle the child if upset, or special words for particular objects, and helps the child feel more secure about their transition into school. The Transition Passport is given to the school SENCO, the class teacher and the specialist teaching assistant (STA).

The home visiting teachers encourage and support the school to give early consideration to the incoming child's needs and to meet with the family to gather information and to start building a positive relationship. They will ensure that any information they hold about the child is passed to the school so that the school can make an application for support from the Foundation Stage Support Team if they feel the child will benefit from additional support from a specialist teaching assistant.

The STAs are informed of their 'new children' for the new academic year ahead towards the end of the summer term when they are also given the passports and all records. This gives them time to liaise with their new school and make arrangements to attend any home visits planned by the school. It also means that they have the summer holidays to read about their child's specific needs and undertake independent research if required.

The Foundation Stage Support Team (FSST)

The FSST provide schools with specialist teaching assistants (STAs) to support the inclusion of young children with special needs, medical needs and disabilities during their transition into mainstream Foundation Stage classes, primarily on entry to nursery, with some support also being allocated to children entering school in their reception year. The Team currently comprises of 34 STAs. The support allows the school or nursery time to get to know the child well, assess his/her needs and plan for how they can best meet their longer-term needs.

Support is sanctioned by a multi-disciplinary panel led by the local authority Special Educational Needs department. Support is allocated for 2.5 hours per session, and is allocated on either a shared or 1:1 basis dependent on need. It can be provided for a maximum period of one year and it is for children who do not have a Statement of Special Needs.

STAs work in partnership with parents, school-based staff and other professionals to support the children to access the Early Years Foundation Stage curriculum. Working alongside the class team on a daily basis, they model good inclusive practice, differentiate activities to support the child's understanding, access and inclusion, maintain daily observation records, deliver speech and language and/or physiotherapy programmes set by therapists, provide progress reports and contribute to planning and assessment.

All support staff participate in a carefully planned INSET programme to increase their skills and knowledge in working with young children with special needs and disabilities in mainstream schools and to provide a model of good inclusive practice. New staff follow an in-depth induction programme that includes training tailored to their specific needs following a core competency assessment, shadowing and team-working alongside experienced colleagues and on-going mentoring and supervision.

A resource kit is issued to every STA, for use in their mainstream placements, to include developmentally appropriate activities for young children with SEN and disabilities, a visual timetable, visual prompts and pictures/symbols. This provides every STA with a set of key resources as a basis to enable the learning and development of the children they support. They will also make additional resources as required when differentiating the curriculum to meet each child's unique needs. This also provides a vehicle to model good practice for school staff, sharing the skills and knowledge required for successful inclusion and optimum educational outcomes.

As the year progresses, part of the role of the specialist teacher is to raise the profile of the supported child with the school senior management team and specifically the SENCO, encouraging discussion and forward planning about the child's longer-term needs. The school is encouraged to think about the provision of support for the following year when the STA will withdraw, so that they can plan for an effective handover.

During the summer term, the STA will make plans with the school to allow the child to start visiting their new classroom on a regular basis, and may make new visual resources, or perhaps a photo book, for the child to take home over the summer to support their understanding of the transition to their next class, dependent on the child's needs.

At the end of each intervention, the STA provides a full report about the child's progress with reference to the Early Years Foundation Stage curriculum and all areas of learning. They will also include any other information that may be helpful, for example with regard to promoting positive behaviour or particular motivators.

In September of the following year, the STA will return to the school to welcome the child back after the long summer break. They will work alongside any new support staff and the new class team for up to a fortnight, supporting the child to settle into their new class and sharing their knowledge and strategies with the new team. Any appropriate resources made for the child the previous year will be left with the school, and the STA will support the new team to make any resources needed.

Planning additional adaptations and training

As soon as the priority places have been allocated, the specialist teacher for FSST immediately checks whether any children have physical needs that may require adaptations, or medical needs that may require additional, specific training. They contact the schools involved and discusses the issues with them directly.

If physical adaptations are required, they will provide all contact details of the relevant local authority department to the SENCo and support them as required to make an application and track the progress made.

If specific training relating to a particular medical need is required, the specialist teacher will liaise with the relevant departments to ensure this is carried out, for example, diabetes pump training, or the care of prosthetic limbs. They will also ensure that the training is not only for the STA, but that the school staff are also trained, so that from the beginning, the school has a full understanding of the child's needs, and feels ownership and shared responsibility for the child, rather than seeing the STA as the only adult responsible for the child's needs. It also ensures that the school can manage the child's needs in the event of the STA's absence. If parents want to participate in the training to share their knowledge, this is also encouraged.

Sleep

There is a growing awareness of the consequences of poor sleep and sleep deprivation, not only for the individual but also for the impact it has on the whole family. This also affects daytime activity and the ability to function fully. However, there is not necessarily a universal understanding or tolerance of children and young people who have not had sufficient sleep. Whilst 40 per cent of children have a sleep problem at some time in their development, up to 86 per cent of children with special educational needs are likely to suffer from disturbed sleep patterns at some point (The Children's Sleep Charity).

Sleep problems can be divided into two main groups: settling problems, where the child has difficulty going to sleep at the appropriate time, and waking problems, where the child wakes repeatedly during the night and cannot self settle. It is also important to remember that puberty can exacerbate sleep problems. As can excessively late bedtimes.

Children and young people with a range of impairments are additionally disabled where their sleep is not sound. It is always worthwhile trying to remove sleep problems that may or may not be related to a disability but can be a source of great stress for the family. Continuity carers and short break providers should replicate family routines that work.

Causes of poor sleep are varied but include light and noise pollution, poor routines and discomfort relating to a disability.

Poor sleep leads to a greater likelihood of:

- mood swings
- anxiety
- obesity and associated risks to the heart
- diabetes
- a greater risk of having an accident
- poor functioning
- less academic success or poorer cognitive development.

It can also lead to poorer concentration, hyperactivity, behaviour that challenges and general irritability.

It's a good idea to encourage parents to keep a sleep diary so that they can keep a track of their child's sleep and identify any unusual patterns, or simply in order that they can evidence what is happening; a sample of a sleep diary is included at the end of this section produced by The Children's Sleep Charity (thechildrenssleepcharity.org.uk).

A number of child development centres and Child and Adolescent Mental Health Services offer support to families around sleep issues where children have challenging behaviour.

Useful contacts

The Children's Sleep Charity. www.childrenssleepcharity.org.uk

Sleep Scotland. A charity providing support to families of Children and Young People with additional support needs and severe sleep problems.
www.sleepscotland.org
Phone: 0131 6511392

Based in Edinburgh but also working in England.

The website has a section on training available to raise awareness of the importance of sleep.

These are curriculum-specific for England, Scotland, Wales and Northern Ireland.

Both charities run courses and work with families individually.

Sleep Diary

The children's sleep charity!

Child's Name:

Date:

Child's DOB:

	Day 1	Day 2	Day 3	Day 4	Day 5	Day 6	Day 7
Any naps during the day? Please note time and duration							
Time bedtime routine started							
Time the child was in bed							
Did you stay or did they self settle?							
What time did they go to sleep at?							
Times they woke up in the night/ how long were they awake/ where did they go back to sleep? Your bed/their bed etc							
Time they woke up in the morning							
Total number of hours sleep							

The Sleep Cycle

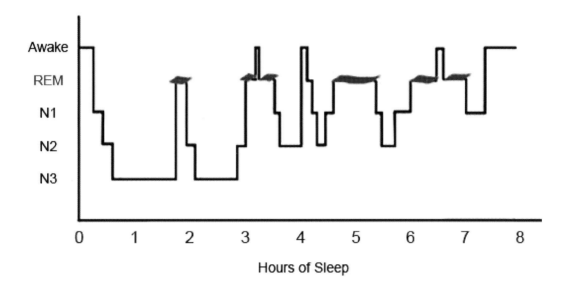

Hours of Sleep

Things that you need to know about your child's sleep cycle:

- Once they are 3 months of age each cycle lasts about 90 minutes.

- Your child is most likely to awake between cycles.

- It takes about 10 minutes for children and older babies to fall into a deep sleep.

- There are 2 types of sleep REM and non REM sleep.

NIFTY©

Ellie Jim

Hello my name is

Ellie Jim

please read my

NIFTY©

It tells you all about
me and my genetic disorder
Neurofibromatosis 1 **(NF1)**

Ellie Jim – Key Facts

- **I am 2 years old, although I look much younger!**
- **I love chocolate**
- **I am half Chinese**
- **I understand more than I can say**
- **I like pretty dresses**

NF1 – Key Facts

- NF1 is a short way of saying neurofibromatosis 1
- NF1 is a genetic disorder that causes tumours in the nervous system
- Affects 1 in 2500 people (that's one baby a day)
- In 50% of cases it is hereditary
- Some people have it mildly and others more severely
- It is a progressive illness and it is not possible to tell how it will develop
- There is no cure

NF1 and me
Here is a list of the most common features of NF1. Mine are indicated!

Café au lait marks (see my pic)	
Cutaneous Neurofibromas (benign skin lumps)	
Optic Glioma (tumours in optic nerve)	
Plexiform Neurofibromas (large benign tumours)	
Skinfold freckling	

Additional Conditions

Here is a list of additional conditions associated with NF1. Mine have a smiley!

Blood Pressure problems	
Chest deformity (see my pic)	☺
Epilepsy	
Learning difficulties	
Bone Problems	
Ptosis (drooping eyelids)	☺
Small stature	☺
Scoliosis	

Learning Disabilities

I do not appear to have any learning disabilities.

However, learning disabilities can occur in up to 60% of people with NF1 and usually do not get picked up until school age.

So please be aware if you think I might be developing a learning disability and let my parents know.

How you can help

1. Because there is an increased risk of developing cancers and neurofibromas please ensure you put a generous amount of a high factor sun block on me on a hot day.

2. Because of my sunken chest I often get food caught under my top please can you check this after lunch so that I am not uncomfortable.

3. Although I am small compared to other children please don't baby me.

What changes do I need to look for?

If you notice any of the following please take me to A and E:

1. Sudden loss of consciousness including fainting

2. Headaches

3. Changes In appearance of a lump, especially rapid increase in size or hardness

4. Unexplained pain

5. Sight difficulties

6. Breathing problems

7. Listlessness

©MMU 2012

6. Promoting a partnership with the child

If a service is to work in partnership with the child, rather than 'doing unto' the child, certain basic principles should be considered and promoted in relation to each child accessing the service:

- **Independence and self-reliance.** All children should be encouraged to take as much responsibility for their own care as they are able to, thus promoting independence and self-reliance.

- **Communication.** Disabled children should have as much say as possible in the way their support is given and therefore their method of communication is an essential element that needs to be understood, documented and shared.

- **Dignity.** The child's dignity and right to privacy should be respected at all times.

Independence and self-reliance

All services should identify the ways in which they are working that will encourage disabled children with high support needs to become more independent and self-reliant in the way their support and care is given.

The report *Managing My Way* (Council for Disabled Children 2011) outlines current government policy, which is based on the principles of 'giving children and young people more choice and control over their care services'. On an individual level better outcomes are achieved when individuals are involved in choosing their services and making decisions about the kind of treatment and care they receive (Department of Health 2006). *Managing My Way* highlights a number of studies that suggest well-informed and supported children and young people can and do take personal responsibility for helping to manage their health and serious medical conditions from a very early age. Apart from any direct health benefits resulting for the individuals, it can increase their wider sense of self-efficacy and control over their lives and futures. Within the context of this publication, this means that wherever possible disabled children should be encouraged to be involved in as much of their care as they can and the staff who work with them should understand their communication so that their care is delivered in a way with which they are comfortable.

Staying Positive is a series of workshops run under *The Expert Patient* programme (Department of Health 2001) for young people living with a long-term health condition. The aim of the workshops is to give the young people the skills to improve their self-management both from a health perspective and in terms of leading as fulfilling and independent a life as possible. The evaluation of these workshops found that young people enjoyed taking part; and their involvement helped them to learn more about their conditions and how to manage their health better. The workshops underlined the importance of medication adherence, but in ways that helped the young people adopt a more positive attitude to something previously seen as burdensome. It had helped them to understand the importance of talking directly to doctors and nurses rather than relying on their parents to do it for them, and had helped them to do so more effectively. After participating in the workshops, young people who were more involved in their self-care reported that their parents seemed more confident and trusting of them to manage their health than before and 'less uptight about letting them go out or being a bit more independent' (Salinas 2007).

There are a number of examples of resources or equipment that have been developed to help children and young people gain more control over their own health.

1. Young Epilepsy, a national charity that campaigns to improve education, health and other services for children and young people with epilepsy in the UK, has published two diaries: one for children between the ages of five and 10 years and the other for young people. The diaries assist children, young people and their parents to keep track of seizures, thus encouraging them to take more control over their own health. The diaries are child friendly, containing jokes, activities and information as well as contributions from over 50 well-known, popular children's illustrators. For the health professional, the diaries provide a more accurate record of the child's seizures.

Young Epilepsy website
http://youngepilepsy.org.uk/all-about-epilepsy/help-and-support/for-children/seizure-diary

http://youngepilepsy.org.uk/all-about-epilepsy/help-and-support/for-teenagers/seizure-diary

2. Walsall NHS Healthcare Trust has developed a leaflet to help young people attend appointments on their own. http://www.councilfordisabledchildren. org.uk/what-we-do/work-themes/health/resources/leaflets-for-going-to-appointments-or-into-hospital

3. In Nottingham, many of the young people with muscular dystrophy have an electronic arm rest which aids self-feeding, rather than being dependent on others to be fed. In addition, many young people with this condition have 'cough assist machines', which help them clear their own secretions instead of having suction.

Communication

Current government policies and guidance encourage all services to consult with children and give them a greater say in the way their care and support is delivered. Giving disabled children more say should happen at a number of different levels and should take into account the child's impairment and method of communication. Taking part in decisions that affect one's life is important at both an individual and public level:

- At an **individual level** children and young people make personal decisions relating to their own care and support. For example, this could include indicating the ways in which they feel comfortable with being lifted, being helped during toileting or where they want to be supported with eating. Most disabled children and young people who need high levels of support are likely to have regular reviews – either within education or social care. They should be helped to give their views through the review process.

- At a more formal or **strategic level** children and young people give their views about the services they use. Participation at a strategic level can take place as one-off, time-limited consultation events, for example a focus group, or as ongoing consultation through the involvement in strategic planning and consultation forums.

Helping disabled children make decisions may often mean that services need to find creative ways of obtaining their views and preferences. The usual decision making process is made up of the following elements:

- **Information** – being given information to understand what has happened or information on which to base a decision (informed choice).

- **Cognitive process** – weighing up different options and making a choice.

- **Expression** – expressing one's decision or views.

- **Action feedback** – receiving acknowledgement or feedback on one's views or decisions or having one's decisions acted upon.

This means that making decisions is affected by:

- comprehension – ability to understand and retain information

- cognitive ability – ability to weigh up information and reach a decision

- communication – ability to communicate the decision made.

For many disabled children and young people with severe learning disabilities this 'usual process' of making decisions may need adapting and simplifying. Services need to find ways of breaking down the elements or doing things 'differently' to ensure that all children can take part in decisions and have a say in the way their support is given.

Disabled children who do not use language to communicate will either use an alternative form of communication (for example, symbols or signs) or will communicate in an individual way through their non-verbal behaviour, gestures and noises. Communicating successfully with severely disabled children is often dependent on getting to know the child rather than on specific methods and technique. A recent study concluded that:

> ... there is clear consensus on one very important point: communication with people with the most complex needs is most successful with familiar, responsive partners who care about the person they are communicating with. (Goldbart and Caton 2010, p.1)

It is incredibly important not to underestimate a child or young person's capacity to participate based on their communication skills. The Council for Disabled Children recently carried out research with children and young people to find out which health outcomes they prioritised. Included in the research were young people who participated using talking mats and who were clearly able to identify and indicate their health priorities (Morris and others 2013).

It is vital that all participation work builds in feedback to young people about what has happened as a result of them sharing their views.

Practical ways of working with alternative communication methods

Information on the child – The admission form or information that services ask parents for must always include details about the child's communication. This information should be recorded and shared with all the staff who support that child. The previous chapter gives an example of an 'All About Me' profile used by a service in Cornwall as well as a description of the NF file, developed by a parent to describe her child who has Neurofibromatosis 1.

Training – Staff or carers may need some training in alternative communication methods, but generally lack of training should not be used as an excuse to exclude children from services. British Sign Language (BSL) is a comprehensive language in its own right, in much the same way as English is. Children using

BSL to communicate will need to be supported by staff or carers who are trained in BSL. However, most other communication methods – Picture Exchange Communication System (PECS), symbol communication, Makaton, electronic communicators – can be learnt by staff or carers alongside the child with a minimum amount of formal, off-the-job training.

Communication passports/profiles – A recent study looking at the most effective ways of communicating with people with profound and multiple learning disabilities (PMLD) describes a communication passport as 'the process of gathering, sharing and making explicit information about the person and their communication acts as an intervention for staff, family members and the community' (Goldbart and Caton 2010, p.8). Information on non-verbal communication should explain how a child indicates their needs (hunger or thirst); how they show their emotions or feelings (happy, sad, distressed or bored); and how to respond to a child and develop a non-verbal conversation or interaction (eye-contact, facing the child; using their sounds).

For disabled children who communicate in an individual way through their non-verbal behaviour, gestures and noises, who are often best understood by those that know them well, using a communication passport to understand their communication is vital. Many disabled children will have a communication passport, written and developed by their school or by a speech and language therapist. It is also important that the child does not have a multiplicity of passports, profiles and plans. It is not important which form is used, but rather that the necessary information on communication is available to all staff and carers working with the child. This information may be included in other documents – such as the All About Me profile included in Chapter 5. The Short Breaks Passport developed in Coventry can be found at the end of this chapter. It contains all the information that a short break carer needs to know about the child as well as their method of communication. Passports can also be valuable for children who are able to communicate but would prefer not to discuss their needs repeatedly with different staff.

If a child does not have a communication passport and that information is not available in some other format, a simple passport can be developed by the service to ensure that all staff understand the child's non-verbal communicative behaviours.

Developing a simple communication passport

A passport details the communicative behaviours of a child. It explains what you think the child means and explains how staff should respond to the child.

The first step in developing a simple passport is to draw up a list of the most important and appropriate needs and feelings that staff in a service need to know in order to support a child – for example, feelings of comfort, distress, hunger, thirst, anxiety, pain.

The second step would be to speak to at least one person, but preferably two or three who know the child well and ask how the child communicates these basic needs – how does the child indicate that they are happy or enjoying something, how do they indicate unhappiness or distress, how do they indicate that they are hungry or thirsty or in pain? For example:

How does the child tell you when they are:	What does the child say / what noise do they make / what sign do they use?	What does the child do with their hands, feet, body language etc. or how does the child behave?
Hungry		
Thirsty		
Comfortable		
In pain		
Uncomfortable		
Like someone		

The third step is to put this information into a passport format. For example:

When I do this	People think I mean	You should do
When I kick my legs out, smile, laugh and blow kisses	I am happy and enjoying what I am doing	I would like you to let me continue what I am doing or do this activity again
When I make a long moaning sound, bite my hand or cry	I am distressed or not enjoying what I am doing	I would like you to stop this activity
When I bang my hand on my leg	I am hungry and would like something to eat	I would like you to give me some food
When I stick my tongue out	I am thirsty	I would like you to give me a drink
When I make eye contact with you	I am showing you that I know you and like you	I would like you to interact with me

Dignity

The child's dignity and right to privacy should be respected at all times. Pr[...] offering a service to a disabled child with high support needs, staff should discu[...] the issues relating to privacy and dignity.

In relation to providing intimate care, this means that before a child starts using a service or attending an activity, staff should identify places where these tasks will be carried out safely and privately. Generally it is agreed that privacy can be respected by allocating one adult to provide intimate care unless there is sound reason for having more than one adult present. Where moving and handling requires two people, it is good practice for the second person to leave the room once the manual handling task is completed and return once the task is finished and the child is re-clothed.

Carers Trust[13] is the largest carers organisation across the UK. It offers the following guidance to its care staff.

When you are involved in the provision of personal care it is important to maintain and wherever possible improve the independence of the child or young person receiving the care. As well as involving the child or young person in all decisions about their care, you should also encourage and support them to help with the care activities themselves rather than increasing dependence by doing everything for them. Never rush the child or young person or take over to speed things up. You could, for example, encourage them to:

- dry themselves as much as possible after a wash
- brush their own teeth if able
- choose their own clothes, activities and meals.

Always provide personal care and support in a way that maintains and respects the privacy, dignity and lifestyle of the child or young person receiving the care. Small things make a difference. For example:

- knock on doors before entering (you are working in someone else's home)
- reduce unwanted physical exposure of the body when assisting with washing by covering the child or young person with a towel
- never talk over the head of the child or young person and make sure they are involved in any conversation you are having
- talk to the child or young person respectfully, value their opinion, take their views into account and respect their wishes wherever possible
- consult the child or young person in matters to do with their own care and enable them to make choices wherever possible.

---

[13] Carers Trust policies cannot be reproduced without permission.

1. *Managing My Way.*
...ildren.org.uk/resources/cdcs-resources/managing-my-
...rces/research-report

The Expert Patient: A new approach to chronic disease
...ry.

Our Health, Our Care And Our Say: A new direction for

Goldbar... ...) *Communication and people with the most complex needs: What works and why this is essential.* Study conducted for Mencap by the Research Institute for Health and Social Change, Manchester Metropolitan University.

Morris, C, Janssens, A, Allard, A and Shilling, V (2014) *Informing the NHS Outcomes Framework: what outcomes of NHS care should be measured for children with neurodisability?* National Institute for Health Research.

Salinas, ME (2007) Evaluation study of the *Staying Positive pilot workshops: A self-management programme for young people with chronic conditions* (unpublished). Department of Primary Health Care, University of Oxford: Oxford, UK.

Resource examples:

Short Break Passport – Short Breaks Team, Coventry Council.

7. Consent

In order to support children and young people who require clinical procedures or moving and handling, parents should be involved at many key stages of the process outlined in this book, for example they should be involved in the risk assessments, care plans, training and reviews. This chapter deals with both parental consent that is required when carrying out a clinical procedure or giving medication to a child or young person as well as children and young people giving consent.

Children and young people giving consent

In terms of age and level of understanding, the child or young person should be involved in indicating their consent to the support they receive. Chapter 6 outlines in detail the involvement of disabled children in the decisions that affect them and the need to ensure that staff are picking up non-verbal communications with regard to how comfortable the child is with the administration of a procedure or intimate care tasks.

Where children and young people are able to give consent, their consent should be recorded. Consent falls under the legal framework of the Mental Capacity Act (2005) and the Family Law Reform Act (1969). Generally the Mental Capacity Act applies to adults (those over the age of 18 years), but it does in part apply to young people aged 16 – 17 years and gives them the right to consent. However, where young people in this age group refuse to give consent, this may in certain circumstances be overridden by their parents or the court. In other words, they have the right to say 'yes' but not the right to say 'no' – as consent can be sought from another source. In relation to children and young people under the age of 16, the Act states that they have the right to take part in consent decisions – in line with their age and level of understanding.

In order to determine whether or not disabled young people can exercise their right to consent, their capacity is assessed. When assessing capacity to make a decision or give consent it must be remembered that it is a 'time and decision specific test' – in other words, the young person may be able to make some decisions and not others, or may be able to make a decision one day but not the following day. Assessing their capacity is based on whether or not they can understand and retain the information relevant to the decision, their ability to use or weigh up that information and their ability to communicate their decision.

If a disabled child or young person does not have capacity to make a decision or give consent then that is generally done by their parents or whoever has parental responsibility. All decisions or giving consent must be done with the child's best interests at the centre of the process.

A flow diagram outlining the process of capacity to consent to treatment is included at the end of this chapter. The same process should be used by services – other than health – when making decisions about the child's capacity to consent to medication and other clinical procedures or whether the parents should give that consent.

Consent from parents

Consent is required in order to carry out clinical procedures or for giving regular medication – whether orally or through an enteral tube. Giving consent may be done in a number of different ways:

- A service may have a specific consent form that covers the giving of medication or undertaking of clinical procedures, which should name the support staff carrying out those procedures. A copy of the form used in Wiltshire is at the end of this chapter.

- Consent to give medication or carry out clinical procedures may form part of a more comprehensive consent form covering a number of different areas of care. A general consent form used by Bleasdale School in Lancashire (school for children with profound and multiple learning disabilities) can be found at the end of the chapter.

- Consent to give medication or carry out clinical procedures forms part of a health plan or short break agreement. At the end of the chapter is an example of the consent form used by the Family Placement team at Leeds City Council. The form brings together a brief description of the procedure, the associated risks as well as the written consent required.

A copy of the consent form should be kept in the child's file and a copy should be given to the parent. If changes are made to the clinical procedures, they should be discussed at the review (described in detail in Chapter 13) and the consent form may need to be altered and signed again.

There are separate guidelines that cover the giving of medication in schools (*Guidance on Supporting Pupils at school with medical conditions,* DfE 2014).

Consent – information sharing

Personal information about children and families held by professionals is subject to a duty of confidence, and should normally not be disclosed without consent. However, the information may be passed to someone else with the individual's consent for a particular purpose, for instance to other professionals involved in their care or treatment or for research purposes.

Where information is shared, there is an implied understanding that the information will not be used except where it is strictly needed to help the professional provide the service. Each member of the team, and any person who provides administrative or secretarial support, has an obligation to treat the information as confidential.

Confidentiality and consent should, where possible, be introduced and discussed with children and young people to ensure they understand their rights (including refusal, withdrawal or partial withdrawal of consent) and staff responsibilities. Personal information on children and young people is ordinarily subject to a legal duty of confidence, and should not normally be disclosed without the person's consent. However, where there are concerns that a child is or may be at risk of significant harm, disclosure of information may be necessary to safeguard the well-being of the child.

Children and young people should, where possible, be made aware of these conditions before giving their consent and all services and organisations should have clear policies in place for staff on how to deal with safeguarding issues.

Capacity to consent

This is a very complex area. Following is a flow diagram that captures the key elements and their implications for capacity to consent. However, this area is underpinned by a number of pieces of legislation, legal precedence and guidance. The key pieces of guidance are the Department of Health publications: *The legal aspects of the care and treatment of children and young people with mental disorder* and *Reference guide to consent for examination or treatment.*

The key pieces of legislation are the Mental Capacity Act 2005 and the Family Law Reform Act 1969.

Is it contemplated that treatment may be given in a psychiatric unit in relation to a mental disorder under the Mental Health Act (MHA) 1983?

Yes → The treatment can be given (even without consent) under the MHA 1983 but consent should still be sought. 1, 2

No ↓

Is the child aged 16 or 17?*

Yes → The child is assumed to be capable of giving consent, but a refusal can be overridden*. If the child is shown to lack capacity to make the particular decision then a 'best interests' decision will need to be made on his or her behalf. This means that whoever is making a decision or taking any action on that person's behalf must do this in the person's best interests.

No ↓

Is the child 'Gillick competent'?
A Gillick competent child is a child who has attained sufficient understanding and intelligence to be able to understand fully what is involved in the proposed intervention.

Yes → The child is regarded as competent to consent to a particular intervention but if they refuse treatment then this decision can be overridden as above.

No ↓

Is the decision within the zone of parental control?
The zone of parental control is not a straightforward concept and clinicians are advised to be cautious about relying on the consent of a parent if there is any indication that he or she is not acting in the best interests of the child.

Yes →

A person with parental responsibility for the child may make the decision on the child's behalf – although this can be challenged by way of an application to the court for a declaration as to his or her 'best interests'.

No ↓

If the decision is urgent then the responsible clinician can give emergency treatment but otherwise consideration should be given to making an application to the court for a declaration as to his or her 'best interests'.

*The law on consent to treatment, including treatment for mental disorder, for young people (aged 16 – 17 years) is governed by the Mental Capacity Act (MCA) 2005 and Family Law Reform Act (FLRA) 1969 s8. The MCA 2005 creates a rebuttable presumption that all individuals aged 16 or over have capacity to make decisions for themselves.

For 16 to 17 year olds, the MCA 2005 presumption of capacity to make decisions has to be considered in the context of FLRA 1969 s8. This provides that persons of this age can consent to any surgical, medical or dental treatment. The courts have, however, distinguished between the right to consent and the right to refuse – and held that in certain cases a court (or even a parent) can override a refusal by such a child (e.g. *Re: R (A minor) (Wardship: Medical Treatment)* (1992)). While it is questionable whether the case law based on FLRA 1969 s8 is still good law (preceding as it did the enactment of MCA 2005), it is nevertheless the case that the courts, in the exercise of their wardship powers, can override certain treatment refusal decisions of 16- and 17-year-olds even if the young person is 'Gillick competent'.

This flow diagram and the following paragraphs are extracted from p.202 – 3 of Disabled Children: a legal handbook (Legal Action Group 2010)© Steve Broach, Luke Clements and Janet Read, available at www.lag.org.uk

A service should have clear guidelines for staff on who should give consent and how that consent is recorded.

Carers Trust[14] –
National Personal Care Procedures states:

CONSENT

1.0 CONSENT FOR CARE
1.1 If a child or young person is competent to give consent for care themselves then it will be sought directly from them. The legal position regarding "competence" is different for children aged under 16 and young people aged 16 and 17.

1.1 Children aged under 16
1.1.1 There is no specific legal age when a child becomes competent to consent to treatment or care; it depends both on the child and the seriousness or complexity of the treatment or care being proposed. Children aged under 16 are deemed competent to give valid consent to care if they have "sufficient understanding and intelligence to enable him or her to understand fully what is proposed" (sometimes known as "Gillick competence").

1.1.2 If a child under 16 is competent to consent for himself or herself it is still good practice to involve their parent / person with parental responsibility in decision-making, unless the child specifically asks you not to and cannot be persuaded otherwise.

1.1.3 If a child under 16 is not competent to make a particular decision, then their parent / person with parental responsibility can take that decision for them, although the child should still be involved as much as possible.

1.2 Young people aged 16 and 17
1.2.1 Once children reach the age of 16 they are presumed in law to be competent to give consent for themselves. This means that in many respects they need to be treated like adults – for example if a signature is required on a consent form they can sign for themselves if able to do so. However, it is still good practice to involve their parent / person with parental responsibility in decision-making unless the child or young person asks you not to.

1.2.2 If young people of 16 or 17 are not competent to take a particular decision, then their parent / person with parental responsibility can make that decision for them, although the young person needs to be involved as much as possible.

1.2.3 When deciding if a young person aged 16 or 17 lacks capacity to make a specific decision, the principles contained within the Mental Capacity Act 2005 can be applied. Please refer to the adult's personal care procedure (B01b) section 4.0 for details.

continued

[14] Carers Trust policies cannot be reproduced without permission.

1.3 'Best interests'

1.3.1 Any decisions taken on behalf of a child or young person who is not competent to take the decision themselves or who lacks the mental capacity to do so, must be taken in the child or young person's best interests, in consultation with their parent / person with parental responsibility.

1.3.2 In some cases multi-disciplinary 'best interest' meeting may be held, comprising professionals involved in the care of the child or young person, their parent / carer / close family members as appropriate. A decision will be made as to the benefits of the proposed care and a resolution made as to how that care will be provided if it is decided that it is in the child or young person's best interests to provide it. The outcome of the 'best interests' meeting will be recorded in the child or young person's file and all necessary information regarding the provision of personal care entered into their care plan.

1.4 Written consent

1.4.1 Crossroads Care requires written consent for all care provided. A model care plan that can be used by schemes and which incorporates an appropriate consent form is available at CT.03.

1.4.2 Written consent can be given by a competent child or young person and / or the child or young person's parent / person with parental responsibility as appropriate.

References used in this chapter

Broach, S, Clements, L and Read, J (2010) *Disabled Children: A legal handbook*. London: Legal Action Group.

Department for Education (2014) *Guidance on supporting pupils in schools with long-term or additional medical needs.*

Department of Health, National Institute for Mental Health in England (2009) *The Legal Aspects of the Care and Treatment of Children and Young People with Mental Disorder: A Guide for Professionals.*

Depertment of Health (2009) *Reference guide to consent for examination or treatment (second edition).*

Care Quality Commission (2011) *A new system of registration, The Mental Capacity Act 2005, Guidance for providers.*

Resource examples:

- General consent form – Bleasdale School, Lancashire.

- Consent and risk assessment for a clinical procedure – Leeds Family Placement Team, Leeds City Council.

- Consent form – Wiltshire Children and Young People's Community Health Care Planning Working Group jointly with SEN Service, Wiltshire Council.

27 Emesgate Lane, Silverdale, Nr. Carnforth,
Lancs. LA5 0RG
Tel: 01524 701217 Fax: 01524 702044
Email: head@bleasdaleschool.lancs.sch.uk
Website: www.bleasdaleschool.lancs.sch.uk
Headteacher: Mrs Kairen Dexter

CONSENT FORM

Name of Pupil: _____

Please indicate permission or otherwise for your child to be involved in the following sections, by crossing out as appropriate. These permissions can be changed at any time by written confirmation to the Headteacher.

Curriculum Areas

Staff assistance provided at all times to support pupils in the following activities

1	Swimming		
	a	Bleasdale School pool	YES / NO
	b	Other pools	YES / NO
	c	Leisure Centres/Fun water parks	YES / NO
2	Outings/Environmental Education		
	a	On foot	YES / NO
	b	In the School's vehicle (ambulance)	YES / NO
	c	Staff vehicle with escort (comprehensive insurance cover in place for members of staff)	YES / NO
	d	Coaches	YES / NO
	e	Staff cars without escort (only if pupil does not require an escort)	YES / NO
	f	Trains	YES / NO
	g	Boats	YES / NO
3	Attendance at college courses/classes		YES / NO
4	Rebound Therapy – on site		YES / NO
5	Rebound Therapy – off site		YES / NO
6	Collective Worship		YES / NO
7	Reflexology		YES / NO
8	Aromatherapy		YES / NO

Therapeutic Provision

1	Vibration Therapy (Not appropriate for some pupils following surgery)	YES / NO
2	Massage sessions	YES / NO
3	Jacuzzi sessions	YES / NO
4	Management of and application of Orthotics by school-employed staff, e.g. corsets, splints, as prescribed by the Health Service to individual pupils	YES / NO

5   Use of specific therapy equipment applied by school-
    employed staff, e.g. walkers, standing frames etc., as prescribed
    by the Health Service personnel   YES / NO

6   Therapy based activities and authorised treatment by
    Therapist for staff to carry out   YES / NO

Care Procedures/Handling Procedures

1   Trimming of toe-nails, fingernails by school-employed staff YES / NO

2   Attendance to personal hygiene of pupils by school-employed
    staff, as part of the pupil's individual care plans under
    strictly controlled procedures   YES / NO

3   Assistance with management of pupils with gastrostomies,
    under nursing direction and supervision   YES / NO

GENERAL

1   Group or individual photographs which may be seen in:

    •   Newspapers or magazines   YES / NO
    •   School & LEA publication   YES / NO
    •   Promotional materials   YES / NO
    •   On School Website   YES / NO
    •   On LEA Website   YES / NO

2   Participation in in-service training courses and workshops

    •   Bleasdale House School-employed staff   YES / NO
    •   Staff from other schools under supervision from School-
        employed staff   YES / NO

3   Medical consultants reports passed to key members of staff
    (strictly limited) to manage requirements for pupils   YES / NO

N.B.   All the above are strictly controlled to preserve the school's integrity and pupils' rights at all times

Please indicate below if there are any other specific areas not outlined above, in which you do not wish your child to participate.

………

………

………

Every effort will be made to ensure pupils' safety at all times in activities undertaken in school time.

Signed: …………………………………… on behalf of: …………………………………………

Print Name: ……………………………… Date Signed: ……………………………………

Received by: ……………………………… Date Received: ……………………………………

Family Placement Medical  Form 1

The Leeds Teaching Hospitals **NHS**
NHS Trust

East Leeds NHS
Primary Care Trust

LEEDS
CITY COUNCIL

FAMILY PLACEMENT CHILDREN'S SCHEME
NURSING PROCEDURES

Identification of Procedure and Parental Consent

1.	Child's Name and Date of Birth *David Wilkinson 26th September 1996*

2.	Name, Address and Telephone Number of Foster Carer who has agreed to carry out the nursing procedure *Jodie Johnson,14 Short Breaks Lane, Pudsey, Leeds*

3.	Name, Address and Telephone Number of Child's Consultant

4.	Name, Address and Telephone Number of Child's GP

5.	Procedure(s) Required Gastrostomy Training for giving medication and water

6.	Parental Consent: I/We give permission for the above Foster Carer to carry out the procedure as agreed above for my child: Signed: Date: Signed: Date:

7. Name, Professional Title, Address and Telephone Number of Qualified Nurse who has trained the carer in the Procedure.

Sharon Wilson, Children's Community Nurse, Leeds Medical Centre.

8. Procedure   Date Taught

9. Signature of Qualified Nurse confirming training has been given:

Signed: Date:

10. Signature of Foster Carer to confirm that they feel competent to carry out this procedure:

Signed: Date:

11. This plan has also been agreed by the following:

i. Family Placement Worker   Signed:

i.i. Family Placement Co-ordinator   Signed:

NURSING PROCEDURE RISK ASSESSMENT

1) Why is this nursing procedure required for this child?

David has a gastrostomy in situ and currently receives water and medication via his gastrostomy. David has previously been prescribed feeds to be given via his gastrostomy as he was failing to thrive. These have been discontinued and David is now having oral supplements.

2) What are the risks if the procedure is not undertaken in respect of the child?

David requires extra fluids to keep him hydrated and to prevent constipation. He requires his Movicol for constipation.

3) Identify any risks for the child associated with this nursing procedure

David's button can get pulled out. This is a negligible risk as he isn't pump fed. Infection of stoma site.

4) How have these risks been addressed?

The carers have been taught that if the button comes out or is displaced (partially out) they either push the button back in and tape down or insert a new button. A spare button is provided when David goes to his carer. If the carer has any concerns they can contact the parents or the named nurse in children's nursing team or Ward 48 at Leeds General Infirmary. The parents have been taught to reinsert the button.

If the stoma site becomes infected the carer should contact the children's nursing team or Ward 48.

5) Who is authorised to undertake this procedure?

The giving of water and medication can be undertaken by the carer trained by Sharon Wilson, the named nurse who knows David.

If the button comes out this can be reinserted by the carer, the parent, the named nurse, or hospital (See Section 4).

6) Outline the review arrangements in respect of this procedure.

It is the responsibility of the carer to contact the nursing team to arrange to be trained (Phone number). Yearly updates are recommended and this again is the responsibility of the carer.

Wiltshire parental consent form

Parental agreement on general administration of medication

Request to supervise the administration of medicines to my child/young person

I confirm that my child / young person .... requires the following medicines to be taken in accordance with medical advice and as detailed in the healthcare plan.

Medicines	Where stored	Time Required	Amount	How given

Names of carers authorised to give medication ....

Please indicate which of the following you would like the support carer/setting staff to carry out:

a   Keep the medicines and assist my child/young person who will take the medication him/herself as detailed above.   YES/NO

b   Keep the medicine and supervise my child/young person to ensure that he/she takes the medicines as detailed above.   YES/NO

c   Keep the medicines only and seek professional assistance in administering them.   YES/NO

If appropriate, please state which professionals will assist: ....

....

In making this request I accept full responsibility for my child/young person's welfare.

I agree that all medicines will be given to the carer in the original container.

Signed (Parent) .... Date ....

Decision by Carer

    a   I am willing/not willing to meet your request   YES/NO

    b   I agree to establish a written record of action taken   YES/NO

    c   *I agree to make arrangements for the storage of medicine   YES/NO

    d   I agree to undergo training to give the above medication   YES/NO

Signed (Carer) …………………………………………… Date ……….................……

Signed (for DCE) …………………………………………Date ……….................……
*Head teacher should sign in the case of a school setting

This consent form could be adapted to include specific clinical procedures, for example:

Type of procedure ………………………………………………….………………

For how long will your child/young person need this to be undertaken?…………

Method …………………………………………………………….………………

Timing …………………………………………………………….………………..

Side-effects ………………………………………………………….……………

Procedures to take in an emergency ……………………………………………

In making this request I accept full responsibility for my child/young person's welfare and consent to the carer carrying out the above healthcare procedure.

Signed (Parent) ……………………………………………. Date …………….…..

Decision by Carer

    a   I am willing/not willing to meet your request   YES/NO

    b   I agree to establish a written record of action taken   YES/NO

    c   I agree to undergo training to administer the above procedure   YES/NO

    d   After appropriate training I agree to administer the above healthcare procedure   YES/NO

Signed (Carer) …………………………………………… Date ……….................……

Signed (for DCE) …………………………………………… Date ……….................……

8. Managing risk through risk assessments

As highlighted earlier in this book, many disabled children and young people find it difficult to access and join in a range of services across education, short breaks, play and leisure because service providers consider their care as posing too great a risk. Yet it is possible to include disabled children with the most complex of support needs, providing services adopt a 'can do' attitude and manage risk effectively. Disabled children with high support needs have the same rights as other children to access services and their rights should always be balanced with the perceived and actual risks.

There are elements of risk involved with many of the tasks carried out to support disabled children who require clinical procedures, moving and handling and intimate care. Many of the risks cannot be removed completely, but it is possible to manage them. Risk management will form the basis of ensuring that these children are included in both specialist and universal services. Where children are supported via a direct payment the same principles of ensuring that risk is minimised apply.

Risk management should cover activities that take place within the usual service or activity building, visits or trips away from the base as well as the home of the child or carer if the service is delivered there.

The purpose of risk management for staff is to ensure that:

- tasks are carried out in the safest possible way
- any risk to staff is minimised.

The purpose of risk management for children is to ensure that:

- they are not exposed to unacceptable risks
- they can take part and enjoy all the activities that other children do.

The elements in risk management

- Risk refers to the possibility of a situation occurring that would involve exposure to danger or a hazard, that is, the possibility of something harmful happening.

- Risk is a combination of the likelihood of something harmful happening and the seriousness of the potential injury.

- A hazard or danger is less likely to cause harm if certain controls are in place. Controls are the steps taken either to eliminate the hazard or reduce the associated risk to an acceptably low level.

- Risk is managed by assessing it, avoiding it if it is unnecessary and reducing it to a level which is 'reasonably practicable'.

- When considering what is 'reasonably practicable' the needs of both the child and staff should be taken into account.

- Reasonably practicable, as defined by the Health and Safety Executive (HSE), means 'an employee has satisfied his/her duty if he/she can show that any further preventative steps would be grossly disproportionate to the further benefit which would accrue from their introduction' (HSE 1992, p.8).

- A key element in any risk management strategy is safeguarding. Risk assessments should cover issues relating to safeguarding, for example intimate care that may be required when carrying out a procedure for a particular child. The assessment should balance both the child's right to be kept safe with the right to be treated with dignity.

In order to manage risk, all services will need to:

- clarify who is responsible for carrying out risk assessments
- detail the training required to carry out risk assessments
- develop the procedures and paperwork required to carry out risk assessments
- agree on arrangements to monitor and review all risk assessments on a regular basis.

While services may draw in professionals from other agencies to help with risk assessments in specialist areas, it is the responsibility of the service to ensure that risk assessments are in place. For example, a youth club would not be expected to undertake the risk assessment on enteral feeding or lifting a child onto pieces of sports equipment, but the management group for that youth club is responsible for ensuring that there is a risk assessment in place. If a local authority is offering a direct payment to a family, the authority should ensure that the parents have the skills to carry out the risk assessments or access to professionals who can help them assess risk and put safeguards in place.

Addressing fears about managing risk

Staff may have concerns about the risks involved to both children and staff in including disabled children in their services, such as the fear they will be blamed if something goes wrong, lack of insurance and inadequate training. These anxieties can be minimised if staff assess all relevant areas of risk, take adequate steps to minimise them and ensure that their actions are 'reasonably practicable'. It is also important to bear in mind that it is the employer who is held responsible and staff are only responsible if they have not carried out the task in accordance with the risk assessment and their training.

'Think safety'

Many larger services employ health and safety officers to carry out risk assessments and, while their role and specialism is vital, all staff working with children should have an awareness of health and safety issues and how to assess and minimise risk.

Good practice in this area indicates that risk assessment and risk management should not rely solely on health and safety officers. Assessments and policies should be written in a way that all staff can understand. The forms and how to assess a new situation should be written in plain English rather than in health and safety jargon. An example from Leeds City Council of a risk assessment completed by a social worker prior to a short break placement can be found at the end of this chapter.

Training staff in risk management is about training staff to think 'safety' rather than training staff to complete risk assessment forms. This will mean that whatever situation staff find themselves in they will feel confident at looking at the situation and identifying the potential risks. Local authorities should make their training available to parents who are employing personal assistants as they will need to develop the same knowledge about management of risk.

Use of equipment

In relation to moving and handling, the controls identified in the risk assessment may recommend the use of equipment. Equipment, while often useful, is not always the solution to every moving and handling situation. In principle, equipment should always encourage and maximise the child's or young person's independence rather than increasing dependency. Staff using equipment should be trained in its usage.

Aisha is a quiet child who loves sparkly and shiny toys and getting messy. She has quadriplegic cerebral palsy with some muscle spasms, uses a wheelchair and is fed through a gastrostomy peg. She currently eye points and uses facial expression to communicate. She was two years old when she started attending Little Breaks in Buckinghamshire, a short break service, managed by Barnardo's providing three hour sessions for disabled children.

Initially when Aisha started attending Little Breaks she was small enough for staff to lift and handle comfortably. However as she became taller and heavier Little Breaks requested support from an occupational therapist to ensure that staff could manage her safely. The occupational therapist carried out a detailed risk assessment of the handling staff would undertake during sessions. As Aisha only attends the session for three hours it was important that any equipment needed was appropriate and not too costly. The occupational therapist recommended the use of a low level wheeled stool to make transfers more comfortable. The service purchased this equipment and it has really helped staff to lift Aisha and ensure that she can continue to be included and enjoy the same activities as the other children.

Equipment is not necessarily all large and expensive – there are small pieces of equipment such as sliding boards and transfer sheets that are relatively inexpensive and are easy to store. Services need to liaise with the occupational therapists already working with the child to identify ways of loaning or obtaining equipment so that the cost of the equipment does not become the barrier to the child accessing the service or activity.

> Little Breaks, following child-specific advice from an occupational therapist, has found that using a simple handling belt, a relatively inexpensive piece of equipment, has enabled a number of children to continue to take part in the activities offered by the service. For example, the belt has been used to support a child who has a weakness on the left side of her body to participate in physical play activities such as using a climbing frame. The belt has given the child a sense of independence while remaining safe in her play.

The general and the specific

Risk assessments will cover general situations as well as situations and tasks that are specific to each child and each procedure. Once a service has received information about a child (described in Chapter 5), the risks specific to that child need to be identified. Individual plans can help staff identify the additional needs of a child and clarify the safety measures that need to be in place.

Clinical procedures

Risk assessments on clinical procedures are likely to be both general and specific. A service may need a general risk assessment on having oxygen in the building and a specific risk assessment relating to the child who requires oxygen. While the service is responsible for ensuring that risk assessments are in place, it is usually the health professional, namely the registered nurse, who will carry out the risk assessments together with service staff.

> The Children and Young People's Training Team, part of Wiltshire Children and Young People's Trust, have developed a risk assessment (at the end of this chapter) that encourages mainstream services to know the questions to ask when considering including children with complex health needs in a range of education, leisure and social care services. From their experience of working with non-specialist health staff, they found that often staff did not know what questions to ask that were relevant to identifying the risks. The risk assessment form, found at the end of this chapter, provides the questions, identifies the information staff need, as well as the training, equipment and support required to safely include children with high support needs.
>
> continued

Only the relevant parts of the risk assessment are completed (with the setting and parents) and once completed with one setting, parents can take a copy with them to other settings. Of course, depending on the activity or setting there will be changes but a lot of the basic information will be the same. The team encourage all settings in Wiltshire to use the same documentation and there has been real progress with this. Not all the medical terminology has been removed from the form because this terminology is likely to be in letters and diagnosis and so it can be helpful to understand the basic terms relevant to a child's condition, but the risk assessment process is about looking at what that medical condition means to managing the child in a particular setting.

The team have had really positive feedback about this process; non-health staff find it an efficient and effective way of learning about some complex health conditions. The accountability for the risk assessment is held by the setting lead but if it is identified that staff will need to carry out clinical procedures, such as administering Buccal Midazolam; the responsibility is with the healthcare professional to ensure that relevant training and support is provided.

CARIN 4 Families is a support service offered in Nottingham and Nottinghamshire by Nottingham Children's Hospital to children who require a high level of healthcare support at home. The support is offered by either a healthcare professional or support worker trained by a healthcare professional to carry out clinical procedures. A risk assessment of the family home (a copy can be found at the end of this chapter) is completed by the nurse prior to the support starting.

Moving and handling

Risk assessments on moving and handling are likely to be both general (e.g. applicable to all the children who use wheelchairs) as well as specific (relate to the particular needs of an individual child). As with clinical procedures, the service is responsible for ensuring that the risk assessments are in place but these should be carried out jointly with the occupational therapists, physiotherapists or back care specialists who know the child and train the support staff. Parents employing personal assistants through direct payments should be given access to professional staff to help them carry out risk assessments on moving and handling. A risk assessment completed by an occupational therapist in Leeds prior to a short break is found at the end of this chapter. This assessment looks at the environmental factors of a short break carer's home and its suitability for the placement of a child who uses a wheelchair.

There is specific legislation and guidance that covers the management of risk in this area. The regulations state that risk assessments should cover:

- the lifting task: why is it required, are there alternatives?
- the child or young person's weight, needs and abilities
- the physical environment
- the individual capacity of the person doing the lifting.

If a service is using equipment – such as mobile hoists – specific risk assessments may need to be carried out on the use of this equipment by a qualified person, such as a physiotherapist or occupational therapist.

> The Specialist SEN Service, part of Wiltshire Council Schools and Learning Directorate, has developed a risk assessment form that informs the moving and handling plan (copies of these documents are at the end of this chapter). A small number of staff from the centrally employed service, who specialise in physical impairment, are trained as manual handling trainers. They work with the Physiotherapy and Occupational Therapy service and the setting – either schools or early years – to undertake the risk assessment, followed by the handling plan. This is sent to the setting or school for them to adopt. This joint agency team then train the school staff as required for the individual child. The Specialist SEN Service also offers a general course in basic moving and handling training for staff working with children in schools and early years settings.

Specific policies

There are areas that have specific regulations and guidance and they are likely to be covered in the employer's health and safety policy and guidance. These areas are:

- storage of medicines
- Control of Substances Hazardous to Health (COSHH) regulations 2002
- clinical waste
- infection control
- fire and evacuation procedures.

Resource examples:

1. Risk assessment completed by a social worker prior to a short break placement – Leeds Family Placement Team, Leeds City Council.

2. Healthcare needs risk assessment – developed jointly by Wiltshire Children and Young People's Community Health Care Planning Working Group and the SEN Service, Wiltshire Council.

3. Risk Assessment – CARIN 4 Families – Nottingham University Hospitals NHS Trust (originally developed by South Staffordshire and Shropshire NHS Foundation Trust).

4. Risk assessment completed by an occupational therapist prior to a short break placement – Leeds Family Placement Team, Leeds City Council.

5. Moving and Handling Risk assessment – Specialist SEN Service Wiltshire Council.

6. Moving and handling plan – Specialist SEN Service Wiltshire Council.

Leeds CITY COUNCIL

Risk Assessment Form PS4 F1   Name of Child: David Johnson   Date of Birth: 20.03.97

SERVICE:	Family Placement		LOCATION:	Leeds

ACTIVITY:	Short Breaks

Responsible Manager:	SW Team manager		Signature:		Date:	xx/xx/xx

Assessment by:	Family Placement SW	Signature:		Date:	xx/xx/xx	Review Date:	xx/xx/xx

What are the hazards?	Who might be harmed and how?	Evaluate the risks. What are you already doing?	What further action is necessary?	Action By Whom?	Action By When?	Complete Y/N (Date)
Are there any risks involving the need for Personal Care?	David, if his personal care is not carried out appropriately. Risks in relation to hygiene, infection, self-esteem and dignity.	David is changed, bathed and washed regularly and appropriately.	The SB Carer to meet David's personal care needs appropriately and respectfully. Parents to provide incontinence pads to carer.	SB Carer Parents	Ongoing for each short break	
Are there any risks involved in feeding the child?	David may choke if given food that is of incorrect consistency.	All food must be chopped finely or mashed and David is to be fed slowly.	SB carer to ensure all David's food is safe for him to eat and he is fed slowly.	SB Carer	Ongoing for each short break	

115

What are the hazards?	Who might be harmed and how?	Evaluate the risks. What are you already doing?	What further action is necessary?	Action By Whom?	Action By When?	Complete Y/N (Date)
Can the child prepare simple drinks and food under supervision to increase independence skills and what are the risks associated with this?	No					
Does the child require any invasive nursing procedures and what are the risks associated with this?	David has a mic-key button gastrostomy for medication and water. This needs to be kept clean and any person administering water and medication must be fully trained. There are risks that the mic-key button may block or fall out	David has his gastrostomy checked and changed regularly by nurses in school. All those who administer water or medication for David are fully gastrostomy trained.	SB carer to be gastrostomy trained, School Nurse will provide training.	School Nurse SB carer	xx/xx/xx	
Does the carer need to administer medication to the child and if so what are the risks associated with this?	Yes, as detailed above.	As above	As above	As above	As above	
If the child administers their own medication what are the risks associated with this?	N/A David is unable to do this.					

What are the hazards?	Who might be harmed and how?	Evaluate the risks. What are you already doing?	What further action is necessary?	Action By Whom?	Action By When?	Complete Y/N (Date)
If the child has a complex medication regime how will this be managed?	David – if his medication is not given his health needs will not be fully met.	All carers made aware of David's health needs and those who will need to administer medication are fully trained.	SB carer to be fully trained to administer David's medication. School Nurse will arrange this.	School Nurse, SB carer	xx/xx/xx	
What are the risks around medication storage?	Medication may be affected if not stored correctly.	Medication to be stored out of reach of children, in a safe place and in correct containers clearly labelled.	Parents will provide medication in correct containers clearly labelled. SB carer will store medication as appropriate.			
Does the child have epilepsy and if so what are the risks associated with this?	No					
Does the child have any other disability or allergy which may have an associated risk factor?	Daniel has cerebral palsy and spastic quadriplegia. David uses a baclofen pump to treat spasms. David suffers from oesophageal reflux. David has learning difficulties and severe communication difficulties.	All who care for David are made fully aware of his needs and how to meet these. David has regular medical oversight from a number of medical professionals.	SB carer to be given all information in relation to David's needs prior to his first overnight short break.	Social Worker	xx/xx/xx	

What are the hazards?	Who might be harmed and how?	Evaluate the risks. What are you already doing?	What further action is necessary?	Action By Whom?	Action By When?	Complete Y/N (Date)
Does the child have any behaviour which is physically challenging?	No					
Does the child have any behaviour which is emotionally challenging?	David can become frustrated by the limitations of his disability. This can cause him upset and distress, impacting on his emotional health and self-esteem.	David is given time to communicate and make choices. Give David positive praise, reassurance and respect.	SB carer to respect David and promote his own ways of communicating in a positive way.	SB carer	Ongoing for each short break	
Does the child have any behaviour which is verbally challenging?	No					
Does the child ever harm themselves or others?	No					
Are there any risks associated with the child wandering or absconding?	David may wander in his power chair when out in the community as he is interested in exploring his surroundings.	David is fully supervised when out in the community, he has a badge with carer's details on in case he gets lost.	SB carer to fully supervise David when out in the community.	SB carer	Ongoing for each short break	

What are the hazards?	Who might be harmed and how?	Evaluate the risks. What are you already doing?	What further action is necessary?	Action By Whom?	Action By When?	Complete Y/N (Date)
Can this child go out alone. If so what safeguards need to be put into place, how far are they allowed to travel from the house, etc?	No					
Is the child vulnerable to abuse (sexual, emotional, physical, neglect)?	As a disabled child David is more vulnerable to abuse and exploitation.	Safeguards are in place to ensure his safety – SB carer is an approved carer with references and CRB checks. David has a multi-agency team of professionals involved to promote his welfare and safeguard him. David has an allocated Social Worker who will be contacted with any child protection concerns.	Continuation of Family Support Plan, sharing of information between involved professionals and parents. Risk assessments in place.	SB carer Social Worker	Ongoing	
What level of supervision does the child require and what are the risks if this is not given? Can they be left alone?	David needs constant supervision though he can be left alone for short periods.	David is supervised at all times and can have short periods where he is left alone with carer remaining at a close proximity (e.g. left in his room to watch TV, regularly checked on).	SB carer to provide this level of supervision.	SB carer	Ongoing for each short break	

What are the hazards?	Who might be harmed and how?	Evaluate the risks. What are you already doing?	What further action is necessary?	Action By Whom?	Action By When?	Complete Y/N (Date)
Are there risks attached to placing this child with other children?	No					
Does the child require assistance with moving and handling?	Yes, David requires assistance for all his moving and handling needs. He is at risk of physical harm if not properly moved and handled.	SB carer has been trained in moving and handling and risk assessment has been completed by Occupational Therapists.	SB carer to ensure David is moved and handled as per advice from OTs. Risk assessments to be adhered to. Any changes to David's moving and handling needs may require re-assessment.	SB carer OT	Ongoing for each short break	
Are there particular home safety requirements relating to the child's disability and have these been addressed?	Yes, carer's home has been assessed by OTs and is safe and suitable for David.	OT assessment and risk assessments in place.	SB carer to adhere to risk assessments and advice from OTs. Any significant changes to David's moving and handling needs will require a re-assessment.	SB carer OT	Ongoing for each short break	

What are the hazards?	Who might be harmed and how?	Evaluate the risks. What are you already doing?	What further action is necessary?	Action By Whom?	Action By When?	Complete Y/N (Date)
Does the child need any specialist equipment and what are the risks if this is not provided?	David needs a wheelchair, power chair, specialist bed, syringe/tubes for gastrostomy, talker, specialist bathing equipment. If David does not have access to the equipment he needs he is at risk of harm.	SB carer's home has been assessed by OTs and is suitable for David. SB carer has been provided with a sling for David.	SB carer to ensure specialist equipment is used appropriately at all times. Any changes to David's equipment needs will require further OT assessment.	SB carer OT	Ongoing	
How does the child travel in the car? Is a car seat required?	David travels in an adapted vehicle in his wheelchair.	David has access to mobility car at home and also uses public transport with support.	If David travels he must be in an adapted vehicle or use public transport.	SB carer	Ongoing for each short break	
Are there any issues for this child relating to bedroom safety? Would there be any risks in room sharing?	No					
Can the child manage money and what are the risks associated with this?	David is able to use money with support and has some understanding of the value.	David to be supported to spend his money.	SB carer to support David to spend his money and understand the value of money.	SB carer	Ongoing	

What are the hazards?	Who might be harmed and how?	Evaluate the risks. What are you already doing?	What further action is necessary?	Action By Whom?	Action By When?	Complete Y/N (Date)
David is a full time power chair user. There are risks associated with the power chair toppling or running over other people.	David may be harmed through power chair toppling or hitting surface/object. SB carer may be harmed through power chair running over her feet.	David is aware that he must take care when using his power chair, he uses a low speed in the home.	SB carer to ensure David adheres to guidance regarding the use of his power chair.	SB carer Young person	Ongoing for each short break	
Date risk assessment updated						
New risks to be addressed						

Wiltshire Children and Young People's Trust Stakeholder Partnership Healthcare Needs Risk Assessment

This form should be completed by the setting in liaison with the appropriate nursing representative and the parents and/or the child/young person. It has been designed to be filled in electronically which will result in the boxes expanding as you type. To fill in a ☒ place the cursor in the box and left click.

Child/Young Person Name:	Date of Birth:
Key worker/Teacher:	Year Group:
Setting:	

Name and role of professionals involved in this Risk Assessment (i.e. Specialist Nurse, School Health Nurse or Community Children's Nurse, Physio, OT, Community Paediatrician):

Date of Assessment:

Reassessment due:

Outcome of Risk Assessment　　　　　**Red ☐ / Orange ☐ / Yellow ☐ / Green ☐**

Comments:

Is an individual health care plan required?　　　　　YES ☐　　　　NO ☐

Signatures

Setting manager/Head teacher:　　　　　　　　　　　Date

Parents:　　　　　　　　　　　　　　　　　　　　　　Date

Young person:　　　　　　　　　　　　　　　　　　　Date

Others involved in completing the assessment:

Section A – Child Information Profile

The phrase 'child' is used throughout this document to represent child or young person.

Summary of Condition/Health Care Needs/Disability:

Is the condition Chronic ☐, Progressive ☐, Life limiting ☐, Life threatening ☐

None of these? ☐

Comments/Areas of Concern including ability to participate in physical activities such as PE sessions, practical lessons or off site trips.

Does the child have any medication which may need to be administered by setting staff?

　　　　　　　　　　　　　　　　　　　　　　　Yes ☐　　　　No ☐

If Yes, please provide a brief summary or complete summary after Section I.

If the child has medication where will the medication be stored?			
Is this location locked but quickly and reliably accessible? Explain:		Yes ☐	No ☐
Where will administration of the medication be recorded and by whom?			
Please note any concerns re: the administration of medication including route, timing, any possible side effects or indications to not administer:			
What is the child's usual method of communication? *(e.g. verbal, gesture, sign language)*			
Does the child have any signs, gestures or phrases that are important for their safety and wellbeing? If Yes please explain:		Yes ☐	No ☐
Is the child generally cooperative? If No please explain:		Yes ☐	No ☐
Does this child have any known mental health problems? If Yes please explain:		Yes ☐	No ☐
How does the child's learning disability affect their communication? Please explain:			
Does this child have a manual handling plan which addresses their handling needs during the administration of medication or treatment? If No, the manual handling plan needs to be updated to include this risk.		Yes ☐	No ☐
Does the child have any chronic pain that is controlled with medication or any other intervention? If Yes please explain:		Yes ☐	No ☐
Does the setting have clear guidance on identifying and managing any chronic pain?		Yes ☐	No ☐
What are the indications when the child is in pain?			
Risk or Hazards/Control measures identified in setting medication policy. (Residual risks will require action to resolve and may result in a Health Care Plan)			

Section B – Airway and breathing

Does the child have any problems in this area? (If No go to next section)	Yes ☐	No ☐

Does the child require support to maintain their own airway?

            Never ☐   Sometimes ☐   At all times ☐

Support required: (Tick all applicable)

Suction: ☐

Oxygen: ☐   Emergency only ☐   Continuous ☐   Dependent ☐

Ventilation: ☐   Invasive ☐   Non-invasive ☐

Tracheostomy: ☐

Basic Life Support: (Tick all applicable)

Nebuliser: ☐   Regular ☐   Occasional ☐

Inhalers: ☐   Regular ☐   Emergency ☐

Other medication/treatments related to airway/breathing:

Does it interfere with any of these activities? (Tick all applicable)

Science ☐   Swimming ☐   Indoor PE ☐   Cooking ☐

Outdoor PE ☐   Outdoor activity ☐   Transport ☐

Does the child have any allergies?	Yes ☐	No ☐

Please give details:

Risk or Hazard/Control measures identified:(Residual risks will require action to resolve and may result in a Health Care Plan)

Section C – Blood/Bones/Joints

Is the child known to have any problems with their blood, bones or joints? (If No go to next section)	Yes ☐	No ☐
Do the child's problems affect bleeding/clotting?	Yes ☐	No ☐

If Yes please give details:

Does the child require regular medication or intervention?	Yes ☐	No ☐

If Yes please give details:

Are there any activities which may need to be modified or monitored to ensure this child's safety?	Yes ☐	No ☐

If Yes please give details:

Risk or Hazard/Control measures identified *(i.e. manual handling or mobility or infection risks)*

Section D – Cardiovascular

Is the child known to have any heart or circulatory problems? (If No go to next section)	Yes ☐	No ☐

Does the child have medication or technology based support for their cardiovascular problems?
Yes ☐   No ☐

If Yes please give details:

Do the child's problems affect bleeding/clotting?   Yes ☐   No ☐
If Yes please give details:

Are there any activities which may need to be modified or monitored to ensure this child's safety?   Yes ☐   No ☐

If Yes please give details:

Risk or Hazard/Control measures identified *(i.e. mobility, participation in activities)*

Section E – Endocrine and metabolic disorder

Does the child have any endocrine or metabolic disorder?
(e.g. Diabetes, congenital adrenal hyperplasia)
if No go to the next section.   Yes ☐   No ☐
If Yes please give diagnosis:

Does the child require medication, monitoring/use of technology?   Yes ☐   No ☐

If Yes please give details including route of administration and equipment required:

Does the child require modification of activities or specific planning prior to undertaking any activities, i.e. PE, Swimming?   Yes ☐   No ☐

If Yes please give details:

Does the child require emergency planning?   Yes ☐   No ☐

If Yes please give details:

Does the child food and drink intake require monitoring?   Yes ☐   No ☐

If Yes please give details:

Risk or Hazard/Control measures identified *(e.g. trained staff available, self administration)*

Section F – Gastrointestinal/Bowel and Feeding needs

Does the child have any gastrointestinal/bowel or feeding problems?   Yes ☐   No ☐
(If No go to the next section)

Is the child able to feed and drink adequate quantities orally?   Yes ☐   No ☐

If yes please explain:

Does the child require any support with eating or drinking (including use of thickening agents or supplements)?   Yes ☐   No ☐

Please explain:

Is there a risk of the child choking?

Never ☐   Occasional ☐   Frequent ☐

Does the child have a **NG, PEG or Gastrostomy button**?　　　Yes ☐　　　No ☐
(Please tick all which apply)

If Yes which does the child require: (Please tick all which apply)

Liquids ☐　　　**Feeding** ☐　　　**Medication** ☐

If Yes are they administered by **bolus or feeding pump**?　(Please tick)

Is the child permitted to take food orally?　　　Yes ☐　　　No ☐
If Yes please explain:

Please identify medications related to gastrointestinal problems and also any medications administered enterally with relevant information:

Does the child have any gut disturbances such as vomiting, diarrhoea, constipation, passing blood?　　　Yes ☐　　　No ☐
If Yes please explain:

Does the child have a colostomy or ileostomy?　　　Yes ☐　　　No ☐
If Yes please explain (including care and facilities needed)

Risk or Hazard/Control measures identified:

Section G – Infection Control/ maintaining skin integrity

Does the child have an infection which requires action to be taken to maintain the safety of the child or others around the child?　　　Yes ☐　　　No ☐
(If No then go on to the next section)

Is the child particularly at risk of infection due to low immunity from immune disorder or treatment which has affected the immune system?　　　Yes ☐　　　No ☐
If Yes please explain:

Is the child known to have an infection or been in recent contact with anyone with an infectious condition (i.e. MRSA, HIV, Hepatitis, Chicken Pox, Tuberculosis, Meningitis, Clostridium Difficile)?　　　Yes ☐　　　No ☐
Please list:

Does the child have any skin conditions which require treatment or management? (i.e. eczema, psoriasis, pressure areas, rashes)　　　Yes ☐　　　No ☐
Please list:

Does the child have medications that need to be administered?　　　Yes ☐　　　No ☐
If Yes please give details (including facilities/equipment required)

Risk or Hazard/Control measures which may be useful in managing any possible risks:

Section H – Neurological

Is the child known to have any neurological problems (i.e. seizures, brain injury or damage, neurological disorder or syndrome)　　　Yes ☐　　　No ☐
(If No go to the next section)

Does the child have history of seizures?
Never ☐   Occasional ☐   Frequent ☐

Please identify type(s) and frequency of seizure including date of last seizure?

Does the child have medication or treatment related to this problem (including rescue medication)?   Yes ☐   No ☐   If Yes please give details:

Are there any warning signs or triggers for a seizure for this child?   Yes ☐   No ☐   If Yes please explain:

Following a seizure what is the child's usual recovery pattern?

Does the child have any other symptoms or problems (i.e. slurred speech, numbness or loss of sensation, ataxic gait)?   Yes ☐   No ☐   If yes please give details:

Risk or Hazard/Control measures identified:

Section I – Urinary and Renal Needs
Does the child require intervention in order to pass urine (i.e. indwelling catheter, suprapubic catheterisation or intermittent catheterisation or Mitrofanoff)?   Yes ☐   No ☐   If Yes please explain:
Does the child have other urinary or renal problems which require monitoring? (e.g. liver problems)   Yes ☐   No ☐   If yes please explain:
Risk or Hazard/Control measures identified:

Risk Assessment Summary

Hazard and possible impacts	Who or what is at risk?	Existing controls in place	Risk rating Red Amber Yellow Green	What additional controls need to be put in place?	Any action points including training needs?	Action point lead person
EXAMPLE ONLY Severe asthma attack	child	Initial training Competency training Availability of medication		Emergency procedures plan updated	Annual asthma updates for staff to be arranged. Annual update of risk assessment	SENCO to contact the School Nurse to arrange

Risk Assessment Action Plan

Health Care need	Frequency	What needs to be in place, e.g. training, facilities for storage and cleaning equipment
e.g. Allergy – seasonal hayfever leading to severe asthma attacks. Antihistamine and inhalers	e.g. Rarely but medication as required	e.g. Staff trained in administration of medication and monitoring of the child. Medication available and stored accessibly when needed. Records of administration kept and shared with parents (as identified in setting Administration of Medication Policy). Individual emergency procedures identified and put in a flow chart. Preventative measures implemented to avoid exposure to allergens.

Risk Scoring

Using the Australia/New Zealand (AS/NZS 4360/1999) risk management standard, which is internationally recognised, a summary of the potential 'grades' of risk issues, based on the risk score, is given below:

Grade	Definition	Risk Score
RED	Extreme Risk	15-25
AMBER	High Risk	8-12
YELLOW	Moderate Risk	4-6
GREEN	Low Risk	1-3

The table represents the possible combined risk scores based on a measurement of both the probability and impact of risk issues. A combination of likelihood and severity score provides the combined risk score.

Probability x Impact = Risk Score
For example where:
Probability = Possible (3)   x Impact = Major (4)   =   Risk Score of 12

This risk score can now be compared to the risk matrix above and a 'colour' or 'grade' can be determined. In the example above, a risk score of 12 would be graded as 'amber' (moderate). Consequently, the employer can then prioritise mitigation actions based on an understanding of the nature of the risk presented.

Individual Risk Scoring Matrices

Probability Matrix

Probability Score	1	2	3	4	5
Descriptor	Rare	Unlikely	Possible	Likely	Almost certain
Frequency How often might it/does it happen	This will probably never happen	Do not expect it to happen but it is possible it may do so	Might happen occasionally	Will probably happen but it is not a persisting issue	Will undoubtedly happen, possibly frequently
Frequency Time-frame	Not expected to occur for years	Expected to occur at least annually	Expected to occur at least monthly	Expected to occur at least weekly	Expected to occur at least daily
Frequency Will it happen or not?	<0.1%	0.1 to 1%	1 to 10%	10 to 50%	>50%

Impact Matrix

Impact Score	1	2	3	4	5
Descriptor	Negligible	Minor	Moderate	Major	Catastrophic
Impact on the safety of client, staff or public (physical/psychological harm)	Minimal injury requiring no/ minimal intervention or treatment. No time off work	Minor injury or illness, requiring minor intervention. Requiring time off work for ≤ 3 days	Moderate injury requiring profess-ional intervention. Requiring time off work for 4 – 14 days RIDDOR/agency reportable incident	Major injury leading to long-term incapacity/ disability. Requiring time off work for >14 days	Incident leading to death. Multiple permanent injuries or irreversible health effects

Nottingham Children's Hospital

Nottingham University Hospitals
NHS Trust

C.A.R.I.N. 4 Families Risk Assessment Pack

Child's name	
Child's Date of Birth	
Address	
Nurse completing assessment Signature Designation	
Date of assessment Assessment completed with	
Proposed date of review	

KEY INFORMATION

LOCATION OF SMOKE DETECTOR	
LOCATION OF FUSE BOX	
LOCATION OF TORCH AND BATTERIES	
LOCATION OF PRP IF APPLICABLE	
LOCATION OF EMERGENCY MEDICATION IF APPLICABLE	
CONTACT NUMBERS FOR PARENT/ GUARDIAN (MINIMUM 2 NUMBERS)	1) 2)
EMERGENCY CONTACT NUMBERS FOR OTHER RESPONSIBLE ADULT	

We are here for you

ACCESS TO AND FROM PROPERTY

- Is the house easily accessible?
- Adequate lighting? – consider winter months, can staff safely get to cars? – consider whether visits should just be in daylight hours if deemed a risk
- Access for emergency services?
- Is there parking outside property/nearby/next street/car park?
- Are there steps/ramps or lifts?
- Any obvious hazards?
- Intercom system? – alarm/gate codes
- Are fire exits clear?

INTERNAL ENVIRONMENT

- Is flooring suitable and intact? – any rugs, uneven floor?
- Stairs – any trip hazards, secure handrails?
- Space for using manual handling equipment
- Food preparation – clean, accessible
- Smoking – ensure families are aware that they cannot smoke in the house when visits taking place – reinforce fire safety if oxygen present in the home
- Noise levels
- Temperature (16 degrees or below not acceptable) – thermal comfort checklist available if concerns about under/over-heating (see reference list for details)
- Room occupancy/overcrowding – see useful resources if concerned

LIVING ARRANGEMENTS

- Current living arrangements for patient
- Family/home dynamics
- Impending changes – building work, moving etc.

MEDICAL EQUIPMENT

- List equipment and service dates/companies who service
- Any other equipment needed?
- Are there enough main sockets for all equipment? – ensure extension leads are not overloaded (see maximum voltage guideline)
- Is any back-up equipment required?
- Plan in case of power failure

NAME OF EQUIPMENT	SERVICE DUE	COMPANY

OTHER EQUIPMENT NEEDED:

LIGHTING, HEATING, ELECTRICAL APPLIANCES

- Visible hazards – sockets and wiring, trailing leads etc.
- Fuse box location – record below
- Heating – any hazards e.g. free standing electric fires?
- Gas fire? Carbon monoxide risk
- Lighting – is it adequate and working? Is there adequate light for when staff are on night shifts? Check lighting or light fittings do not present a hazard
- Power company – ensure they are aware if child has ventilator/ concentrator

Fuse box location:

FIRE SAFETY

- Plan for exit in case of fire – detail below
- Smoke detectors – detail location below
- Smoke alarms – tested and working?
- Clear exits that can be easily opened
- Consider if community fire safety team need to be contacted – Tel: provide contact number if possible
- If visits to take place at school/nursery check fire details

Smoke detector location(s) – Record on front of pack also:

WASHING/BATHING/SHOWERING

- Current facilities
- Complete manual handling risk assessment
- Arrange OT/Physiotherapist input as needed

EMERGENCY PLANS

- Does the child have a Personal Resuscitation Plan? If so where is it kept? Ensure all carers are aware
- Are Local Ambulance Services aware of child?
- Plans to go to specific ward?

PETS

- Any pets? Are they well controlled?
- Where are pets to be kept during visit?

PERSONAL SAFETY AND LONE WORKING

- Any obvious risks for lone staff? Consider two person visits to improve safety
- Mobile phone coverage
- Access to landline
- Access to keys to lock doors
- Personal alarms
- Lone working policy available for staff to access on Intranet
- Bleep and on-call support available
- Up to date staff details with on-call
- PPE available i.e. gloves, aprons

STAFF FACILITIES

- Hand washing facilities
- Toilet facilities
- Fridge/drink making facilities
- Explain staff breaks

STAFF TRAINING

- What training is needed for carers?

OTHER ISSUES/CONCERNS

- Any issues we need to be aware of i.e. MRSA, other infectious diseases?
- Does the parent/guardian/any other family member that may be present during the visit have any health concerns they would like us to be aware of i.e. epilepsy, diabetes in case of emergency?
- Any medications with dangerous side effects or risks to certain members of staff i.e. pregnant or trying to conceive?

Managing risk through risk assessments

Risk Assessment Form

Risk Assessor:_____ Date of assessment:_____

Location:_____

Step One – Summary of risk

Step Two – Who is at risk and why?

Step Three – Evaluate risks and identify current controls	A-Objectives	
	B-Harm	
	C-Experience	
	D-Service Delivery	
	E-External	
	Likelihood	
	Risk Score (Highest Score A-E x Likelihood)	
	Priority Indicator Score	

RISK RATING OF 20 AND ABOVE TO BE ESCALATED TO BOARD OF DIRECTORS
RISK RATING OF 10 OR ABOVE NOT LIKELY TO BE ACCEPTED BY TRUST

Step Four – Action Plan		
Proposed Actions	Target Date	Completed

Step Five – Review Date: _____

Risk rating after review:_____

Responsible person(s):_____

Consequence and Likelihood Matrix

	Objectives / Financial	Degree of Harm (to Patient, Visitor or Member of the Public)	Claims & Complaints / Patient Experience / Outcomes	Impact on Service Delivery / Business Interruption / Projects	Adverse Publicity / Reputation / Inspection / Audit / Enforcement Action	Likelihood
1 Minor	Minor impact on Trust objective. AND / OR Barely noticeable reduction in scope or quality AND / OR small loss.	Minor injury not requiring first aid or no apparent injury / adverse outcome, Near Miss.	Verbal locally resolved Complaint. Reduced quality of patient experience not directly related to the delivery of patient care. Small claims (up to £25,000)	Negligible impact, brief loss / interruption > 1 hour of service. Insignificant cost increase / schedule slippage <1%	Local interest, rumours within Trust. Little effect upon staff morale. Small number of minor recommendations, which focus on minor quality improvement issues. Minor non-compliance with Standards for Better Health	Not expected to occur for years. Probability <1%
2 Moderate	Temporary non – compliance with Trust Key Tasks AND / OR Minor reduction in quality / scope AND / OR Loss > 0.1% of Trust budget	Temporary Minor Injury / Illness / Effect. First aid treatment needed, referral to A&E / OH / GP	Justified formal complaint. Unsatisfactory patient experience directly related to patient care readily resolvable	Local only. Some loss / interruption delays in service provision (> 8 hours) < 5% over budget / schedule slippage	Local adverse publicity, local media coverage, adverse publicity for < 3 days. Minor effect on staff morale/public attitudes. Internal inquiry reported to local committee structure. Recommendations made which can be addressed by low-level management action. Non-compliance with the Developmental requirements of the Standards for Better Health	Expected to occur annually in the UK or 1-5 years in the Trust. Probability 1-5%. The event may only occur in exceptional circumstances
3 Serious	Temporary non-compliance with Trust Primary Objective AND / OR Reduction in scope or quality. AND / OR Loss > 0.25% of Trust budget	Semi-permanent injury, Over 3 day reportable injury. RIDDOR / Agency reportable	Independent review. Mismanagement of patient care, short term effects (<1 week). Justified complaint involving lack of appropriate care. Significant claim (up to £250,000)	Critical Service loss / interruption, minor delays > 1 day. 5-10% over budget / schedule slippage	Local media coverage, adverse publicity for > 3 days. Significant effect on staff morale / public perception of organisation. Internal inquiry reported to external agency. Challenging recommendations that can be addressed with appropriate action plan. Reduced rating. Non-compliance with core requirements of the Standards for Better Health	Expected to occur at least annually. Probability 6-20%. The event may occur at some time
4 Major	Non-achievement of Trust's Key Tasks AND / OR Loss > 0.5% of Trust budget	Major injuries, or long term incapacity / disability, Major Specified Injury (RIDDOR)	Ongoing National publicity. Regional inquiry. Ombudsman. Serious mismanagement of patient care, long term effects (>1week). Multiple justified complaints. Multiple claims or single major claim (over £250,000)	Critical Service loss, major reduction in service > 1 week 10-25% over budget / schedule slippage	National media coverage, adverse publicity for < 3 days. Regional inquiry. Severe effect on staff morale, public confidence in organisation undermined. Enforcement action Low rating / Critical report Major non-compliance with core require-ments of the Standards for Better Health	Expected to occur monthly. Probability 21-50%. The event will occur at some time
5 Catastrophic	Non-achievement of Trust Primary Objective(s) AND / OR Loss > 1% of Trust budget	Death or major permanent incapacity	Full National Inquiry. Select Committee. Public Accounts Committee. Totally unsatisfactory patient outcome or experience	Total loss of Critical Service or facility. > 25% over budget/ schedule slippage	National/international media coverage with adverse publicity for > 3 days. Loss of key staff. Public inquiry / MP concerns raised in Parliament. Court enforcement. Non-compliance with legal requirement, which may result in prosecution. Zero rating. Severely critical report	Expected to occur at least weekly. Probability > 50%. The event is expected to occur in most circumstances

Management action

The risk score obtained determines whether the risk is unacceptable, tolerable or acceptable and there are different processes to follow depending upon this score. Please see below as a basic guide and refer to the NUH Risk Assessment Tool (Version 3, 2009) for a more detailed explanation.

Risk Rating	Level at which the risk must be reported	Who needs to be informed	Management Actions Required
Significant (20-25) Unacceptable	Risk Management Committee/ Directors' Group (DG)	Trust Board	Immediate action required to eliminate or manage risk.
High (15-19) Unacceptable	Appropriate Committee of the Risk Management Committee	Risk Management Committee/ DG	Urgent action/senior management attention required to eliminate or reduce the risk.
Moderate (10-14) Unacceptable	Directorate	Organisational Risk and Patient Partnership Committee	Action/senior management attention required to eliminate or reduce the risk.
Low (4-9) Tolerable, manageable	Specialty/ Department	Directorate	Action if cost efficient to reduce or manage risk.
Very Low (1-3) Acceptable	Specialty/ Department	Directorate	Manage situation with routine procedures at a Specialty or Department Level.

Parent/Guardian

By signing you are agreeing that all details in the risk assessment are correct and that you will notify your child's named nurse/bleep on-call as appropriate if there are any changes to this. It is important that this risk assessment is kept up to date to ensure the safety of your child and the staff providing care to your child during visits.

Risk assessment agreed by parent guardian

(Sign and Date):_____

Risk assessment agreed by named nurse

(Sign and Date):_____

Family Support Workers

Please read the risk assessment and speak to named nurse if there are any questions or concerns. By signing you are confirming that you have read and understood the risk assessment and will work within the guidelines set. Also, you must notify the named nurse or on-call as appropriate if there are any changes to this.

Sign	Date	Initial

Guidelines for completing risk assessment pack

The C.A.R.I.N. 4 Families risk assessment pack has been designed to help with the identification and management of risk. This must be completed fully before any visits can take place by family support workers. All details to be discussed with families and signed to confirm this. Once completed, all family support workers who care for the child should read and sign also.

Fill in all sections of pack using prompts to guide you. If any areas are identified as potential risks a risk assessment form (page 8) should be completed – more individual sheets are available. Score the risk using the Consequence and Likelihood Matrix (page 9). Any risk over 20 should be communicated with the board of directors. The Trust will not accept a risk score of 10 and above. This may mean that two person visits might be needed or that it is unsafe to provide visits in a particular environment.

Ensure you detail the proposed actions and then re-score. Risk assessments should be reviewed annually or before if needed due to change in circumstance etc. All risks should be communicated with the Team Leader for C.A.R.I.N. 4 Families.

Contact risk assessment advisor for trust on:

Acknowledgements

Laynton-Bennet, C and Mcclelland, M (2010) *Community Support Team Risk Assessment Pack: New Referral and Current Provision.* South Staffordshire and Shropshire Healthcare: NHS Foundation Trust Nottingham University Hospitals (2009) *NUH Risk Assessment Tool.* Version 3. Nottingham: NUH.

Useful resources

Workplace health, safety and welfare: A short guide for managers
http://www.hse.gov.uk/pubns/indg244.pdf

Measuring thermal comfort
http://www.hse.gov.uk/temperature/thermal/measuring.htm

Children and Young People's Social Care
Child Health & Disability Occupational Therapy
Roundhay Road Area Office
79 Roundhay Road
Leeds LS7 4AA

SPECIALIST EQUIPMENT AND ADAPTATIONS FOR FAMILY PLACEMENT
OCCUPATIONAL THERAPY REPORT

Carer: Rabia Hussein

Address:

Phone:

Child Assessed for Placement: Shireen Khan

Therapist: Mary Fuller (OT)

BACKGROUND

A referral was made to Occupational Therapy by Family Placement to request an Occupational Therapy assessment of the specialist equipment and adaptations needed to accommodate Shireen Khan with family placement carer Rabia Hussein.

ASSESSMENT

Environmental Assessment of Carer's Property

The house is a 4 bedroom detached property. Rabia had a son with muscular dystrophy who passed away last year as a young adult. The house was adapted for Rabia's son approximately 7 years ago to provide a ground floor bedroom with en-suite bathroom. The property is wheelchair accessible to the ground floor. There is a ramp to the main entrance and level access off the kitchen and ground floor bedroom into the garden. The ground floor bedroom has space for a specialist bed (although there is none in place at present) and there is ceiling tracking from the bed area to the bath. The bath is a standard bath set high on a plinth with a bi-fold changing stretcher and over bath shower. There is additional tracking in the lounge.

Suitability of Property to Meet Child's Needs

Shireen has Spastic Cerebral Palsy and is a wheelchair user. She is unable to stairclimb and is lifted for most transfers. The property would be accessible to Shireen, provide a ground floor bedroom and hoisting for essential transfers. Shireen has not been hoisted but it has been identified she is likely to require this soon, especially for bath transfers.

OCCUPATIONAL THERAPY RECOMMENDATIONS

In consideration of Shireen's identified needs and the accommodation Rabia is able to offer, the placement of Shireen with Rabia is recommended as a suitable match.

There are some issues that require attention (as detailed within the recommendations below).

The following issues will require clarification as this placement opportunity is fully explored:

- **The stairs:** The stairs in the hallway are open with no newel posts or banister rails in place. Although there would be no need for Shireen to go upstairs it has been suggested by her physio that she may develop skills to attempt to stairclimb. Shireen would be at significant risk of harm if she attempts to climb the open staircase. Rabia prefers the stairs open but identifies the potential hazard and is agreeable to having these closed in. Rabia has stated however that she would prefer to have spindles rather than a solid block of wood to maintain light in the hallway.

- **The ramp:** The outside ramp was installed several years before the internal adaptations and will need repair in due course. There is evidence of weather erosion and the surface is deteriorating in places. If care is taken the ramp is not unsafe but it is likely that with further bad weather and regular use the ramp will become pot-holed, uneven and unsafe. If Shireen is placed with Rabia this repair will need to take place in the future.

- **Tracking:** The tracking hoists in both the bedroom and lounge need servicing.

- **Childproofing:** Rabia raised the issue of childproofing generally in the kitchen as she is concerned that Shireen might open cupboards etc. The OT would recommend that at least one cupboard is child proofed for storage of bleach/cleaning products etc.

- **Bed:** Shireen is able to transfer in/out of her bed with assistance.

- **Bathing:** As the bath is on a plinth hoisting will be required for bath transfers. This is ideal for Shireen and tracking is already in place. Shireen has not been hoisted yet and the OT would need to carry out a sling assessment with her and potentially work with Shireen to make her feel at ease with hoisting (as she can be nervous when she feels unsteady). A suitable bath support will also be needed for Shireen.

To discuss the contents of this report or if further information is required please contact me on 0113 368 XXX.

Signed: Mary Fuller (OT)   Date:

SCHOOLS & LEARNING DIRECTORATE
Specialist SEN Service

MANUAL HANDLING RISK ASSESSMENT

Pupil Name:	Tilley	
School:	The Crescent Primary	
Physiotherapist:	Alison	
Occupational Therapist:	Sue	
Advisory Teacher:	Hilary	
Date of last assessment:	14.12.10	
Date of this assessment:	13.9.11	
Next assessment due:	September 2012	
Signature		Headteacher
Signature		Physio
Signature		O.T.
Signature		Advisory Teacher

Is a Handling Plan required?   YES   NO

Names of staff trained to carry out Handling Plan:
Leslie
Stuart
Denise

(Full details of each person's training are detailed in the pupil's individual Handling Profile.)

143

Pupil Information

Age: 6

Weight: 71kg on 01/09/11

Body Shape: (underlined)
Tall   <u>Medium</u>   Short
Thin   <u>Average</u>   Obese

Disability:
Spastic quadraplegia
Communication difficulties

Level of dependence:
Totally dependent
<u>Needs assistance to transfer</u>
<u>Some sitting balance</u>
Unable to weight bear on legs
Minimal active participation
Needs some assistance
Full sitting balance
<u>Able to weight bear in standing</u>

Equipment normally used:
Manual wheelchair,
electric wheelchair,
R82 wombat chair,
wheelie stool,
standing frame,
walker,
changing couch,
2 steps stools.

Has a hoist been considered?
       <u>Yes</u>   No

If inappropriate please state reason:
not required yet.

Understanding and compliance:

<u>Age Appropriate</u>   <u>Co-operative</u>
Limited   Unco-operative
Not known   Unpredictable

Handling constraints – pupil

Pain: none known

Spasm: unpredictable movements

Epilepsy/Fits:

Head Control: can support head but unpredictable jerky movements

Fear: startle reflex

Fatigue: will tire easily

Fragility:

Sensory Loss: none known

History of falls or 'Sinking': Yes   <u>No</u>

Other considerations:
Tilley has difficulty controlling her movements and her balance and co-ordination are affected. Although she has little verbal communication her understanding is good – and it is important that she is addressed in an age appropriate manner, consulted and given choices wherever possible.

(A =Life threatening B = Serious injury C = Minor injury 1 = Likely to occur 2 = Could occur 3 = Unlikely)

| Activities Undertaken | Level of Risk | | Control measures to reduce risk |
	Pupil	Helper	(See Handling Plan for existing procedures)
Stand <-> floor	C2	C2	Independent with support of adult or furniture. Close adult supervision – adult to use wheelie stool
Chair <-> stand	C2	C2	Adult assistance – encourage active participation
Standing	C2	C2	Can stand independently against furniture or supported at waist – adult use wheelie stool
Walking	C2	C2	Use walker – close adult supervision
Floor <-> chair	C2	C2	Crawl to chair then encourage to pull to stand – adult assistance at waist if necessary encourage to step round and sit back in chair
Chair <-> chair	C2	C2	Assistance of trained adult – use procedures demonstrated
<-> wheelchair	C2	C2	Assistance of trained adult – use step if required and procedures demonstrated
<-> standing frame	C2	C2	Assistance of trained adult – use procedures demonstrated
<-> transport			Wheelchair transport may be required for trips and excursions
<-> swimming pool	N/A		
<-> hoist	N/A		
Moving about floor	C2	N/A	Tilley can play and move about the floor independently. It has been agreed with her mother that she will not generally wear her helmet when she is on the floor in the classroom but will wear it in PE or for other activities if staff feel it is advisable. Adult supervision
Manoeuvring wheelchair	C2	C2	Adult assistance – Tilley can assist with the brakes and manoeuvre short distances
Manoeuvring electric wheelchair	B2	B2	Adult supervision and verbal prompts to concentrate on task. Move about at walking pace. Power off when stationary
Descending stairs	N/A		Fully accessible site
Ascending stairs	N/A		Fully accessible site
<-> toilet	N/A		

<-> changing table	C2	C2	Lower couch to same height as chair, position chair with brakes on so Tilley can stand on footplate and step round to sit on couch
Maintaining standing for changing	N/A		
Moving around classroom	C2	C2	'crawl' or use walker – encourage independence
In the playground	C2	C2	Use walker, buggy, wheelchair, or free movement as appropriate
In PE/games lessons	C2	C2	Tilley should have access to an adapted PE curriculum. 1:1 support. Wear helmet when out of chair
Changing for swimming	N/A		
Changing for PE lessons	C2	C2	Change in chair – wear jogging bottoms
Out of school trips	C2	C2	Specific RA should be carried out prior to trip. Plan in advance and liaise with her mother to ensure that Tilley can be fully included
Participating in practical lessons	C2	C2	
Carrying school bags	C3	C3	On chair
Moving specialist equipment		C2	Use good handling techniques as demonstrated on basic MH course

Working environment	Level of Risk High / Medium / Low	Control Measures
Uneven, slippery floors	High	Avoid
Variation in level of floor and work surface	Medium	
Extremes of temperature/humidity	Low	
Repetitive action	Low	
Poor lighting	Low	
Space constraints	Medium	Organise classroom and plan working environment

Other Factors: Tilley's dribbly causing her shirt or sweatshirt to become damp. She wears sweat bands on her wrists and will respond to verbal prompts to swallow and also to wipe her mouth. Her mother will provide a spare clean sweat shirt, neck scarves and spare wrist bands so that these can be changed when necessary – this is particularly important in cold weather.

PUPIL HANDLING PROFILE

Pupils Name: Leon

Class: Miss Y

School: The Usual Academy

Physiotherapist: Sue

OT: Jane

Advisory Teacher: Alison

Date of this review: 1 Sept 2013

Signed _____

Head teacher or Representative

Signed _____

Person with parental responsibility

Signed _____

Person completing profile

Date for next review: Sept 2014 or before if his needs change or the ability of his staff changes.

The Manual Handling Regulations (1992) require any handling of children and young people to be formally assessed for risk of injury before a task is undertaken. This is in addition to staff undertaking an informal risk assessment each time before carrying out a handling task. In order to support schools to fulfil this duty, the Physical Impairment service has agreed to assist with the production of this risk assessment. The plan must be signed on completion to be formally adopted by the school and must be updated as per the regulations. All staff involved with manual handling activities should have received basic manual handling training.

Pupil Information

Age: 11 years 6 months

Weight: 36 kg on 30/08/11

Body Shape: (underlined)
Tall   <u>Medium</u>   Short
Thin   <u>Average</u>   Obese

Disability:
Dystonic Quadriplegia

Level of dependence:
<u>Totally dependent</u>
Needs assistance to transfer
Some sitting balance
<u>Unable to weight bear on legs</u>
<u>Minimal active participation</u>
Needs some assistance
Full sitting balance
Able to weight bear in standing

Equipment normally used:
Wheelie stools
Changing table
Liko hoist
Liko silhouette slings size M
Silvalea sling
Powered wheelchair with manual base

Has a hoist been considered?
      <u>Yes</u>   No

If inappropriate please state reason:
not required yet

Understanding and compliance:

<u>Age Appropriate</u>   <u>Co-operative</u>
Limited   Unco-operative
Not known   Unpredictable

Handling constraints – pupil

Pain: occasional but currently in his hips

Spasm: linked to CP + strong startle reflex

Epilepsy/Fits: none

Head Control: limited

Fear: gets tight when uncertain. Startle reaction to sudden noises

Fatigue: yes

Fragility: no

Sensory Loss: uncertain

History of falls or 'Sinking':   Yes   <u>No</u>

Other considerations:

Assistance required

Movement Task		Amount and Type of Help Needed
STANDING	Stand <-> Changing table	Using hoist and Silvalea sling. 2 trained adults required. From standing Leon should be encouraged to turn himself and sit on the side of the couch but will need adult help with this. With one adult to support him, in particular his head, he is lowered sideways so that he is lying on his side on the couch. His legs can then be lifted onto the couch and the sling released. The couch and his positioning can now be adjusted.
	Chair <-> stand	Using hoist and Silvalea sling. 2 trained adults required. Space is essential.
SUPPORT	In standing	In prone stander or using Silvalea sling in hoist, with long handles in place so Leon can hold onto them for support. 2 trained adults required.
	In walking	Using hoist and Silvalea sling. One adult to guide hoist, other to guide Leon's legs – using wheelie stool to avoid stooping.
	Toileting	Leon is changed on the changing table. 2 adults required for hoisting using Silhouette sling. Leon should come to school sitting on his sling.
TRANSFERS	All manoeuvres	The hoist must be used for all transfers. 2 trained staff required at these times.
MOBILITY	In all areas of the school	Leon has a powered wheelchair with hi-low facility which he will use through the school. Leon can propel this chair himself or the chair can be controlled by the adult from behind. He will need supervision at all times, particularly where space is limited.
STEPS AND SLOPES	Descending / Ascending	Steps must not be negotiated. Close supervision on slopes.
OTHER	In practical lessons	Leon finds it easier to use his arms when in the prone stander. 1-1 support required. Appropriate seating is required for the adult so they do not stoop
	In PE/Games lessons	1-1 communication and planning is essential to ensure suitable equipment is available to enable Leon to participate and staff are not put at risk.
	Hydro	Into and out of the pool using the Silhouette sling. 1 member of staff on the pool side and one in the water with Leon.
	Sensory room	Leon will require hoisting to and from the floor. Staff will also need to use a slide sheet to help reposition Leon once on the floor. NB the hoist must not be used on the floor mats.
	Out of school trips	All trips must be individually assessed. He will require 1-1 at all times and 2-1 for any transfers.
	Fire evacuation	Leon must have an individual evacuation plan which should include TA support.

Teaching Assistants and Training

Assistant	Training	Date Trained	Trainer
Myra	Basic Patient Handling	8/07/11	Specialist SEN Service
	Equipment: a) Prone Stander	04/09/11	Sue
	b) Hoist	05/09/11	Alison
	Other		

Assistant	Training	Date Trained	Trainer
Carolyn	Basic Patient Handling	8/07/11	Specialist SEN Service
	Equipment: a) Prone Stander	04/09/11	Sue
	b) Hoist	05/09/11	Alison
	Other		

Assistant	Training	Date Trained	Trainer
Libby	Basic Patient Handling	18/05/11	Specialist SEN Service
	Equipment: a) Prone Stander	04/09/11	Sue
	b) Hoist	20/09/2011	Alison
	Other		

Alison Patrick is a member of the Wiltshire Specialist SEN Support Service and holds current accreditation from Centaur Training as a trainer for Manual Handling.

9. Plans

For children with higher levels of need, the overarching plan is a statement or education, health and care plan. From September 2014 statements of SEN will be replaced by education, health and care plans (EHC plans). The majority of the provisions in relation to EHC plans remain broadly the same as for statements. The threshold for an EHC plan is the same as for a statement – effectively that a school is unable to meet a child or young person's special educational needs. However, a plan may continue up to the age of 25 if the young person is in further education or an apprenticeship. Plans will also continue for 16 – 17 year olds if they are not in education, employment or training. The EHC plan sets out a child or young person's special educational needs, their aspirations, views and interests, the outcomes sought for them and the special educational provision, healthcare provision and social care provision required.

Alongside a child's statement or EHC plan may sit a number of specialist plans. Local practice will differ from one area of the country to the next. In some places children will have separate plans to cover each area of specialist support – for example a healthcare plan, an emergency plan, a moving and handling plan etc. In other regions, a child will have a single plan and where additional support is required this information will form a part or module of that single plan. The arrangement will usually have developed in a specific way due to historical and practical factors in each area of the country.

The important issue is that if disabled children require additional assistance in specific areas of care, the information explaining how the support should be given needs to be written down and shared with all those who are offering this support. Each child should have an individual plan that is specific to their needs. Plans will vary in length and complexity, depending on the needs of an individual child. All plans will be read and used by a range of staff so they should be written in non-jargon, non-medical language that is easy to understand. It is important that arrangements made via personalised budgets where the parent is the employer should use the same plans as directly provided services. The partnership arrangement developed in a geographic area should detail the format of plans to be used.

If disabled children are in foster care or use overnight short breaks, the use of plans to cover their care and support is outlined in statutory guidance. (*The Children Act 1989 Guidance and Regulations. Volume 2: Care Planning, Placement and Case review; and Short Breaks Statutory guidance on how to safeguard and promote the welfare of disabled children using short breaks* DCSF, 2010.) Disabled children receiving overnight short breaks under Section 17 (Children Act 1989) require a 'child in need plan' and for those having overnight short breaks under Section 20, where regulation 48 applies, a 'short break plan' should be written. There is no set template for either of these plans, but the information to be covered is stipulated in the guidance. This means that where disabled children with high support needs are using short breaks, the information covering the specialist support required may be in the form of a single plan or the child may have a 'short break plan' plus a number of specialist plans. Details of templates that can be used are on the Council for Disabled Children website: http://www.councilfordisabledchildren.org.uk/resources/cdcs-resources/short-breaks-training-materials/model-short-breaks-care-plans

The group of disabled children covered by this publication may require healthcare plans – containing their clinical procedures as well as the medication they use. Some children will also have moving and handling plans, as well as emergency plans. As outlined above, these plans may be separate documents or may form a part or module of a single plan.

The healthcare plan

A healthcare plan should adopt a holistic approach detailing all aspects of the child's condition, as well as the medicines and support required and set out:

- particular procedures that should be carried out, including who should do them and the training they can expect

- a backup plan should the person who will usually carry out the procedure be absent

- protocols for exchanging information between agencies (with clearly defined lines of responsibility and named contacts)

- additional risk assessments required for that particular child – who is responsible for carrying them out

- any special healthcare needs that may affect the child's use of services such as transport or play activities, implementation of therapy programmes etc.

- the use, storage and maintenance of any equipment

- information on the manner in which the child prefers any task to be carried out, in order to ensure consistency of approach across all settings the child attends

- any anticipated changes in the child's condition or care routine

- arrangements for reviewing the plan

- parental wishes for the child

- any arrangements for the provision of education or associated services when the child is too unwell to attend school or is in hospital or another healthcare setting.

How should a healthcare plan be drawn up?

- Prior to the child starting at a service a meeting should be held to draw up the healthcare plan.

- The purpose of the meeting is to identify the child's needs and draw up a plan which will support the child in that setting.

152

- All individuals who hold key information on the child should be invited to contribute to the meeting. The meeting should be multi-agency.

- Parents and, where appropriate, the child (depending on the age and understanding of the child) should be invited to take part in drawing up the healthcare plan.

- Information already acquired should be used rather than expecting parents to give the same information over and over again to different services.

- The plan should be agreed by the various agencies that have contributed, and signed by the parents.

- Healthcare plans should be 'live' documents that can be altered, in writing, if the child's needs change. There should be agreement as to who can alter the plan. Changes to health procedures or medicines would need to be made by the appropriate healthcare professional.

- The healthcare plan should be reviewed regularly. If a child has a statement of special educational needs/EHC plan, the healthcare plan should be reviewed at the time of the annual review or more frequently if the child's needs change.

Agreeing healthcare plans across all agencies

It is preferable for a child to have one healthcare plan that is agreed by all agencies and services working with the child. This will provide greater consistency across all agencies and services. It is particularly useful for smaller services as very often they do not have the staff resources and expertise to write their own plan.

Access to the healthcare plan

The healthcare plan should be kept in a place that is accessible to staff, but which takes into account the need for confidentiality. This may mean that protocols for dealing with emergencies are referred to in the healthcare plan but are kept in a place that can be accessed in an emergency.

There are two specific healthcare plans at the end of this chapter. The first is the risk assessment and plan written for children on long-term ventilation using a hydrotherapy pool developed by the specialist nurse at the Rainbows Hospice. The second is a plan, developed in Leeds, covering how to feed a young child who is at risk of aspirating. The plan has been drawn up as a placemat so it is available and visible at mealtimes.

Moving and handling plans

All children with moving and handling needs should have a detailed plan before they start going to a service or activity. The plan should cover all the activities the child may engage in while attending. This should include transfers, toileting arrangements, going on outings, transport and so on. The plan should be clear and detailed enough to be understood by anyone who needs to use it. New regular activities should be added to the plan. The plan should be regularly reviewed and updated.

Very often a plan follows the risk assessment and is drawn up by a physiotherapist, occupational therapist or back care specialist. An example of a moving and handling plan, following a risk assessment used in the education service in Wiltshire, can be found at the end of Chapter 8.

At the end of this chapter is an example of a moving and handling plan for a young person receiving short breaks with a family-based carer in Leeds. A plan covering intimate care forms part of the Good Practice Guide, developed in Sussex, and can be found on page 9.

Emergency healthcare plans

The Council for Disabled Children has worked with the Royal College of Paediatrics and Child Health to develop guidance on producing emergency healthcare plans (EHP) for children with complex healthcare needs and/or life-limiting conditions to make communication easier in the event of a healthcare emergency. This guidance states that emergency plans need to:

- be drawn up after open and sensitive discussion between child, parents or carers and lead health professional, usually the consultant paediatrician

- take into account the views of the multidisciplinary team who know the child best, including the general practitioner

- keep the child's best interests paramount at all times

- be brief so that information can be communicated quickly in an emergency

- use simple language, free from jargon and abbreviations, so that they can be understood by those without medical training

- show clearly what action should be taken so that this can be understood immediately in a crisis situation

- be signed in ink by the lead clinician – usually the consultant paediatrician.

The guidance recommends that the emergency plan should cover:

- Active health concerns.

- Current treatments and medication, which can be included or signposted. The weight (dated) of the child upon which doses were calculated is helpful as a reference point. There should be a clear statement reminding those reading the EHP that treatment may have changed since the plan was written, so all treatment should be confirmed with the family and core health team before being administered.

- Guidance as to what to do if the child is unwell, including any scenarios that might be predictable for that child.

- A clear statement about agreed levels of care should a health emergency occur that makes it crystal clear that resuscitation and life support are appropriate (or not). Some local ambulance services will require a DNACPR (Do not attempt cardiopulmonary resuscitation) form in addition to an EHP for individuals of any age whose EHP includes a statement to allow a natural death.

- Space for an option for the child to be conveyed to hospital for assessment before deciding on the level of treatment appropriate for the situation.

- Agreed 24 hour emergency contact number, for example: on-call community children's nursing service, or on-call paediatric team. If the child's usual paediatrician is the emergency contact, a back-up number for an on-call service should also be given.

- Contact details for parents or carers and any key health professionals who should be contacted in the event of a healthcare emergency.

- The child's postcode as this is often the identifier used by the ambulance service rather than the child's name. It may be necessary to also include postcodes for short break carers and school, especially if these are in a different ambulance service's area.

- A statement about arrangements for review, and who to contact if there are concerns or questions about the EHP or the child's healthcare.

www.councilfordisabledchildren.org.uk/ehp

Children should have one emergency plan, which stays with them wherever they are and is used by all the services and activities they attend. Where staff will be required to administer medication in an emergency – for example, when a child has a seizure – it is important that the information they need is with the child or is easily accessible and is written in a format that is easy to understand, cannot be misinterpreted and can be followed at a time of crisis. Using a flow chart format is often helpful in these situations.

An emergency plan used by Hertfordshire Community NHS Trust is included at the end of this chapter.

In addition to the emergency plan, services need to consider how they deal with emergencies in terms of managing a group of children or the impact that an emergency may have on the other children.

Summon assistance in an emergency

There are a number of examples of creative ideas used in order for a teacher or playground staff member to summon assistance if he/she is alone in a classroom with a group of children and there is an emergency involving one child. The idea behind these systems is to send another child to summon help carrying an easily identifiable object rather than relying on them to carry a verbal message. The two examples given here are:

- a card alert procedure recommended by the Learning Trust in Hackney

- the helping hand system recommended by the nurses responsible for medical needs in the Birmingham South Central CCG.

The card or object needs to be consistent and familiar to all staff across the setting.

The card alert procedure: A warning card is available in the classroom to alert any member of staff to the information they may need relating to a specific child. An SOS card is available in the classroom and held by lunchtime and playground staff, which in the event of an emergency is given to another child to take to a designated place – usually the school office. The staff in the office will respond by ensuring that medication and a trained person are taken to the emergency situation.

The helping hand system: A large cardboard hand (about 20 inches in height) is kept in each classroom, with the name of the class printed on it. In the case of an emergency, another child is given the hand and sent to a designated place – usually the office. The 'hand' is obvious because of its size and it's easy to see and respond to the child carrying it.

Services should all have first aid policies and procedures in place that cover all emergencies.

First aiders must complete an approved training course. The main duties of a first aider are to:

- give immediate help to casualties with common injuries or illnesses

- when necessary, ensure that an ambulance or other professional medical help is called.

References used in this chapter

Department for Children, Schools and Families (2010) *Short Breaks: Statutory guidance on how to safeguard and promote the welfare of disabled children using short breaks* https://www.education.gov.uk/publications/standard/publicationDetail/Page1/DCSF-00183-2010

HM Government (2010) *The Children Act 1989 Guidance and Regulations. Volume 2: Care Planning, Placement and Case review.* https://www.education.gov.uk/publications/standard/publicationDetail/Page1/DCSF-00185-2010

Resource examples:

1. Risk assessment and care plan – Developed by Helen Kenny, Respiratory Specialist Nurse, Rainbows Hospice for Children and Young People, Leicestershire.

2. Placemat – Leeds Family Placement Team, Leeds City Council.

3. Moving and Handling Plan – Leeds Family Placement Team, Leeds City Council.

4. Protocol for the Management of Epileptic Seizures – Hertfordshire Community NHS Trust.

Risk Assessment – Rainbows Hospice

Assessor's Name:	Job Title:	Date:	Assessor's Signature:
Counter Assessor's Name:	Job Title:		Countersignature:

Activity	Hazards (remember – the potential to harm)	Risk L M H	Control Measure (What can be done? Can you eliminate the hazard?)
.... has a tracheostomy and is ventilated and requires special care when using the hydrotherapy pool.	That .... inhales water via tracheostomy	H	1. Ensure there are at least two people in the pool with ...., one to support position in the water keeping airway clear of the water, and one to provide activities. One of these should have completed the pool training. 2. Ensure one member of staff is available on the side to provide assistance and perform suction if required. 3. Check that .... tracheostomy tube is securely fixed and tapes are not too loose. 4. Ensure that .... emergency tracheostomy bag is present and fully stocked and that all emergency equipment is available, including a bagging circuit connected to an oxygen supply. 5. Perform suctioning of tracheostomy if required. 6. Check the suction machine is fully charged with sufficient suction catheters and gloves. Do not have it plugged in to the mains supply. 7. One member of staff should have a clear view of .... at all times to ensure that he/she is not lowered too far into the pool which would allow water to enter his/her tracheostomy. They must inform the staff in the pool immediately so that .... position is raised. 8. If water enters ...., this is an emergency situation and the

	H		
That .... ventilator becomes disconnected resulting in a respiratory emergency.		1. Ensure that ventilator has a long dry circuit in situ and that the ventilator is positioned on a dry surface away from the edge of the pool. The ventilator should be running on battery supply, with batteries fully charged. Check batteries for cracks, chips or breaks which will mean they are not waterproof. 2. Check that the ventilator tubing is fitted securely to the tracheostomy and will not fall into the water. 3. If .... ventilator tubing becomes disconnected from the tracheostomy but it does not fall into the water, the bagging circuit should be attached to the tracheostomy and manual bagging performed and .... removed from the pool and the ventilator reconnected once they are out of the water. 4. Whilst .... is in the water, constant observation should be made of colour, chest movement and any indication of respiratory compromise. If these occur .... should be immediately removed from the water.	emergency alarm should be activated at the poolside. .... should be immediately removed from the pool and placed on the trolley. Suction should be applied to the tracheostomy to remove any water present and hand bagging with 100% oxygen initiated. An ambulance should be called to arrange immediate transfer to hospital. Wet clothing should be removed and warm dry towels used to keep .... warm.

Review date:	Date reviewed:	Manager/ Health & Safety Officer's signature:

Rainbows Hospice for Children and Young People

CARE PLAN

Name: DOB

Date:

Problem
.... has a tracheostomy and is ventilated and requires special care when using the hydrotherapy pool.
Goal
That .... is able to use the hydrotherapy pool safely.
Actions

1. Ensure .... is appropriately dressed to use the hydrotherapy pool.

2. Ensure there are at least two people in the pool with .... one to support position in the water keeping airway clear of the water, and one to provide activities. One of these should have completed the pool training.

3. Ensure one member of staff is available on the side to provide assistance and perform suction if required.

4. Check that .... tracheostomy tube is securely fixed and tapes are not too loose.

5. Ensure that .... emergency tracheostomy bag is present and fully stocked and that all emergency equipment is available, including a bagging circuit connected to an oxygen supply.

6. Perform suctioning of tracheostomy if required.

7. Check the suction machine is fully charged with sufficient suction catheters and gloves. Do not have it plugged in to the mains supply.

8. Ensure that ventilator has a long dry circuit in situ and that the ventilator is positioned on a dry surface away from the edge of the pool. The ventilator should be running on battery supply with batteries fully charged. Check batteries for cracks, chips or breaks which will mean they are not waterproof.

9. Check that the ventilator tubing is fitted securely to the tracheostomy and will not fall into the water.

10. .... should be transferred to the poolside on a trolley in preparation for hoisting into the pool. At least two members of staff should be ready to receive ....into the pool; one member of staff remaining at the side of the pool is responsible for guiding the ventilator tubing, which should not become too wet.

11. One member of staff should have a clear view of .... at all times to ensure that he/she is not lowered too far into the pool which would allow water to enter his/her tracheostomy. They must inform the staff in the pool immediately so that .... position is raised.

12. If .... ventilator tubing becomes disconnected from the tracheostomy but it does not fall into the water, the bagging circuit should be attached to the tracheostomy and manual bagging performed and .... removed from the water and the ventilator reconnected once they are out of the water.

13. If water enters .... tracheostomy, this is an emergency situation and the emergency alarm should be activated at the poolside .... should be immediately removed from the pool and placed on the trolley. Suction should be applied to the tracheostomy to remove any water present and hand bagging with 100% oxygen initiated. An ambulance should be called to arrange immediate transfer to hospital. Wet clothing should be removed and warm dry towels used to keep..warm.

14. Whilst .... is in the water, constant observation should be made of colour, chest movement and any indication of respiratory compromise. If these occur .... should be immediately removed from the water.

15. Initially limit .... time in the pool to approximately 15 minutes building up to a maximum of 30 minutes as he/she tolerates it.

16. Do not take .... into the pool if secretions are particularly loose and he/she is requiring frequent suctioning episodes as this will increase the likelihood of water entering his/her tracheostomy.

17. Do not take ....into the pool if he/she appears unwell or secretions are copious and thick. The increased humidity and movement will increase the likelihood of a secretion plug blocking his/her tracheostomy which will require an emergency tracheostomy change.

18. At the end of the hydrotherapy session ....should be removed from the pool and dried promptly, wet clothing removed and dry clothing applied. Tracheostomy tapes should be changed and dressing applied if used.

Name: _____   Signed: _____

Review Date: _____

Drew's Table Mat

Photo
(child or favourite food)

Updated [INSERT DATE]

Positioning

- Make sure that Drew is upright, stable and comfortable in his wheelchair. Ensure straps in place.
- Encourage Drew to keep his head up and facing forwards.
- Feeder should sit opposite Drew.
- Drew is better facing the dining room with his back to the wall so that he doesn't have to turn to look around.

Utensils

- Drew may be better with a plastic spoon as he often bites on it, although he may choose a normal metal spoon.
- Napkin for catching mess.
- Drew drinks from a normal cup, water bottle or valved straw.
- Try to reduce distracting things in front of him.

Food

- Drew needs modified food that doesn't require much chewing.
- Food consistency should be mashed or finely chopped soft food coated in sauce, gravy, custard or yoghurt.
- Avoid hard lumps, food with skins, stringy food or sticky foods that could stick to the roof of the mouth. Avoid mixed consistencies (eg: lumps in a runny sauce).
- Drew should be offered snacks that dissolve (e.g. quavers) or are very soft (eg: small pieces of very ripe peeled fruit, sponge cake).

Communication

- Drew chooses his own dinner by eye-pointing or using his talker.
- Drew will say "Yes" and shakes his head for No.
- Natural relaxed conversation.
- Tell Drew what you are doing, but avoid comments about how he is managing the food.
- Drew expresses what he wants and when he wants it. Give Drew lots of choices. He will tell you when he is full.
- Drew is easily distracted and this is when he is most at risk. Avoid lots of chat and laughter when he has food in his mouth.

Independence

- Drew is spoon-fed his food.
- Drew should be fed slowly at his own pace.
- Place food into the centre of his mouth.

- Drew will open and close his mouth around a spoon. If he bites down on the spoon wait for him to release it.
- Drew can take small bites of soft snacks (e.g. sponge cake) using his front teeth.
- He manages food using up-down jaw movements. His tongue moves forward and backward, but does not easily transfer food from side to side. Prompt Drew to chew his food rather than swallow whole.
- Sometimes food gets stuck at the sides or roof of Drew's mouth.
- Always check before giving more.
- There may be some food loss, which should be wiped away gently and discreetly every now and again.

Drinks

- Drew drinks small sips of normal liquid.
- Drew enjoys milkshakes and smoothies.

Preferences

- Drew has strong ideas about what he likes & dislikes.
- Drew really likes chocolate, milkshakes, yoghurt, icecream and cheese.
- Drew doesn't like hot spicy food, mint or rice.

Important /additional information

- Drew is tube-fed fluids.
- Drew's weight is monitored regularly. He should be offered high calorie meals. Full-fat butter, cream, cheese, etc. may be added.
- Mealtimes should always be pleasurable and relaxed. Drew benefits from gentle encouragement to eat, but avoid putting on too much pressure.
- Be familiar with the signs of aspirations – speak to the Speech and Language Therapist if you have any concerns.

Signs of Aspiration

Aspiration is when food or drink goes "down the wrong way" i.e. into the lungs.

This can be silent – with no cough. As this is a serious risk to health, everyone involved with the child's feeding should be aware of the signs.

~ Loss or change of colour, e.g. face goes pale / grey / blue / reddens
~ Eyes watering or increased blinking
~ Facial expressions or grimacing, indicating anxiety / distress
~ Coughing
~ Gagging
~ Difficulty or change in rate of breathing
~ Breathing becomes noisy
~ Repeated attempts to clear throat
~ Wet / gurgly / rattly voice quality
~ Runny nose and increased drooling
~ Hiccoughing
~ Lips/nail beds tinged blue
~ Frequent chest infections / pneumonia

IF YOU THINK A PUPIL MAY BE ASPIRATING…

- STOP giving food / drink
- Give them time to recover
- Seek help if still concerned – call first aid trained staff
- Report any concerns to the class teacher

Moving & Handling Care Plan

Child's Name: David Johnson   **DOB: 20.03.02**

Care Plan For: **Short breaks with a carer, Gina Smith**

General Note:

David will be hoisted for all transfers at Gina's. Gina has ceiling tracking hoist in the bedroom/bathroom and lounge to accommodate this. *David should arrive at Gina's from school sitting on one of his black slings. David should have his other black sling with him for bathing.* Gina has a slip-fit sling that can be used in an emergency if David comes back not sitting on his sling.

Transfers:

Chair to bed:
- David should park his wheelchair under the tracking hoist adjacent to the bed.
- David's chair needs to be put in manual override to enable it to be manoeuvred as necessary.
- The pommel with control joystick needs to be removed.
- The bed should be brought up to a good working height for Gina.

If David has <u>not</u> come home on his black sling:
- Fold back the lateral supports on David's chair and undo x2 lap straps. Slip the blue slip-fit sling down David's back as far as possible, leaning David forward to assist.
- The chair can be tilted back to assist in maintaining David's posture while he is without lateral support.
- Slide the leg pieces under each leg, paying attention to David's posture. Once the leg pieces are underneath David they should be crossed over, threading through each other at the base.
- The hoist can then be brought over and the carry bar lowered.
- The sling should then be hooked up to the hoist using the longest loops at the shoulders and legs and the shortest or middle loop for the middle straps (ensure the same both sides).
- Ensure the wheelchair brakes are on.
- David should be lifted slowly off his chair, checking that the back of the sling is underneath his bottom and he is not at risk of sliding out. If the sling is not supporting David enough he should be lowered back down and the sling re-adjusted before trying again.
- David can then be hoisted onto the bed and the sling removed.
- Take off wheelchair brakes to wheel out of the way.

If David comes home on his black sling:
- David can wheel into the bedroom under the tracking hoist adjacent to the bed.
- The bed should be brought up to a good working height for Gina.
- David's chair should be put in manual override.
- The pommel/joystick control should be removed from the chair.

- David's lateral supports should be folded back and both lap belts undone.
- The chair can be tilted back to assist in maintaining David's posture while he is without lateral support.
- The position of the sling should be checked.
- The loops within the material pommel should be pulled out and the leg section straps threaded through it.
- The waist strap on the sling should be fastened.
- The hoist should be brought over and the straps fitted to the carry bar.
- The longest loops should be used for both shoulder and leg straps and the middle (orange) loop used for the middle strap.
- Ensure wheelchair brakes are on before lifting David with the hoist.
- There is no aperture in the black sling but check his positioning before moving away from his wheelchair onto the bed.
- Take off wheelchair brakes and wheel out of the way.

Hoisting back into the chair:
- Position the wheelchair tilted back under the tracking.
- Ensure brakes are on the wheelchair.
- Once David is lowered into the chair ensure his bottom is to the back.
- Pull the lateral supports back into place and fasten x2 lap straps.
- Leave the black sling in the chair, folding back straps etc out of the way.

Bathing:
- David should be hoisted from the bed through into the bath.
- David can be left in his sling for bathing.
- After his bath David should be hoisted out and onto the changing stretcher to be dried and dressed.
- David's 2nd black sling can then be used to either hoist David into bed or back into his wheelchair.

The Lounge:

At home David spends a lot of time on the sofa with his mum. As David is unable to maintain sitting balance, his mum uses cushions to position him on the sofa. David has also now been provided with a Jupiter chair at home that is more comfortable than his wheelchair but provides the support needed to maintain his sitting balance. Obviously it is not practical for this chair to be available for short breaks.

If David wishes to come out of his wheelchair at Gina's to sit on the sofa, there is ceiling tracking in place that can be used for hoisting David from his wheelchair (using the above technique). This was not trialled during the hoist training due to time restrictions. If Gina experiences any difficulties with this an OT can revisit to explore this further.

Care Plan written by Occupational Therapist

Signed:…………………………….........................……Date:………...............………

Agreed by Gina Smith (Family Placement Carer)

Signed:…………………………….........................……Date:………...............………

PROTOCOL FOR THE MANAGEMENT OF EPILEPTIC SEIZURES
Joanna Davidson

1.   BACKGROUND

1.1   Joanna has been diagnosed with epilepsy. She has occasional seizures, and may require support and possibly rescue medication during a seizure. In the past, her seizures have been noted to occur:
• To be completed by parents/clinician

1.2   Joanna's seizures may be preceded by one or more of the following:
• To be completed by parents/clinician

1.3   Joanna's seizures included the following features:
• To be completed by parents/clinician

1.4   The arrangements set out below are intended to assist Joanna during a seizure, to provide safe care for her and to reduce the risk of possible injury.

2.   PROCEDURE FOR DEALING WITH A SEIZURE

2.1   If Joanna has a seizure the following procedure should be followed.

If possible lay Joanna gently on the floor (or a soft mat if immediately available) and place her in the recovery position and loosen any tight clothing around her neck area. Remove any furniture that may pose possible risk of injury.

2.2   Gently hold Joanna in the recovery position. Reassure and comfort her. Restraint to her limbs, head or torso should only be used in order to prevent Joanna from injuring herself. It may be appropriate to place a blanket or rolled up jumper/jacket under her head.

2.3   Note the time that the seizure commenced.

2.4   In general, Joanna's seizures tend to last for no more than two or three minutes. After this she may wake, still be feeling sleepy but seem to be recovering. Her mother should be telephoned at this point, and may wish to collect her from school and take her home.

2.5   If Joanna is still seizing after five minutes or if following the cessation of a first seizure, she begins to seize again without making a full recovery from the first seizure:

- an emergency ambulance should be called on 999
- her mother should be called on (parent's telephone numbers to be inserted – home and mobile)
- she should be given 10mg/1ml of Midazolam (Epistatus) using the oral syringe provided in her emergency pack. The medicine should be squirted gently between her gum and cheek and, following administration, her lips should be held gently together in order to stop the medicine dribbling back.

2.6   When the ambulance staff arrive, tell them what has happened including details of the medicine that has been given and the time that it was given. They will probably want to take the residue of Midazolam with them for verification.

2.7   A written record should be made that the medication has been given.

Summary Chart

If/When Child's Name starts to seize ('fit')

- If Child's Name is not already on the floor, gently lay him/her on the floor in the recovery position

- Comfort, reassure and talk to him/her

- Remove any furniture etc. from the immediate area in order to reduce possible risk of injury

- Loosen any 'tight' clothing around Child's Name's neck area

- Note the time that the seizure commenced

- Hold him/her gently in the recovery position

- If seizure ceases within two to three minutes, telephone his/her mother who may wish to take him/her home from school to complete her recovery

- If either;
  a) Child's Name continues to seize for five minutes or
  b) Child's Name begins to seize again without having made a full recovery from the first seizure
     - Call an emergency ambulance '999'
     - Call his/her mother by telephone (to be inserted)
     - Administer 10mg/1ml of Midazolam (Epistatus) using the provided syringe into the space between his/her gums and cheek – gently hold his/her lips together

- When the ambulance staff arrive, tell them what has happened including details of the medicine that has been given and the time that it was given

- No further doses of medicine should be given. A written record of any medicines given should be made

10. Training

For staff to be able to carry out any clinical procedure or assist a child requiring moving and handling they will need general training as well as child specific training. Training staff in intimate care may be at a general level only. The same applies to support workers or personal assistants who are employed through direct payments or other forms of personalised budgets. This chapter will look at training in the three different areas covered separately in this book. This separation is for ease of understanding; in practice many of these children may need support and trained staff to meet their needs in all three areas.

Clinical procedures

Many services, particularly larger ones, may undertake general training for all staff, which will give them a good understanding and knowledge of certain more common conditions. For example, all staff in a school may attend general training on epilepsy that will cover the need for rescue medication, but only those working with children who require rescue medication will receive child specific training on administering the medication.

Training on a specific clinical procedure will need to be carried out on an individual basis for a specific child. This training cannot be 'cascaded' by one member of staff attending a course to other members of staff, nor can training around one child be generalised to another child. In general, staff supporting disabled children who require clinical procedures are unlikely to have any health qualifications and are not usually registered nurses. Training on a clinical procedure MUST be carried out by a registered nurse or medical practitioner (community paediatrician). Although it is good practice to invite parents to attend the training, parents cannot train the support staff. This applies to support staff employed by the parent using direct payments or other forms of personalised budgets.

In June 2005 the Royal College of Nursing (RCN) developed an advisory list of procedures that may be safely taught and delegated to unregistered health and non-health qualified staff following a child-specific assessment of clinical risk. This list appears on the RCN website and is regularly updated as medical procedures change and develop.

Permitted tasks:

- Administering medicine in accordance with prescribed medicine in pre-measured dose via nasogastric tube, gastrostomy tube, orally or applied to skin, eyes and/or ears.
- Injections (intramuscular or subcutaneous). These may be single dose or multiple dose devices that are pre-assembled with predetermined amounts of medication to be administered as documented in the individual child's care plan (preloaded devices should be marked when to be administered, e.g. for

diabetes where the dose might be different am or pm. In many circumstances there may be two different pens, one with short-acting insulin to be administered at specified times during the day and another for administration at night with long acting insulin).

- Inserting suppositories or pessaries with a pre-packaged dose of a prescribed medicine.
- Rectal medication with a pre-packaged dose, i.e. rectal diazepam.
- Rectal paraldehyde that is not pre-packaged and has to be prepared – permitted on a named child basis as agreed by the child's lead medical practitioner i.e. GP or paediatrician.
- Administration of buccal or intra-nasal Midazolam and Hypo stat or GlucoGel.
- Blood glucose monitoring as agreed by the child's lead nursing/medical practitioner, i.e. GP, paediatrician or paediatric diabetes nurse specialist.
- Assistance with inhalers, cartridges and nebulisers.
- Emergency treatments covered in basic first aid training, including airway management.
- Tracheostomy care, including suction using a suction catheter.
- Emergency change of tracheostomy tube.[15]
- Oral suction with a yanker sucker.
- Assistance with prescribed oxygen administration, including oxygen saturation monitoring where required.
- Administration and care of liquid oxygen administration including filling of portable liquid oxygen cylinder from main tank.
- Ventilation care for a child with a predictable medical condition and stable ventilation requirements (both invasive and non-invasive ventilation). NB: Stability of ventilation requirements should be determined by the child's respiratory physician and will include consideration of the predictability of the child's ventilation needs to enable the key tasks to be clearly learnt.
- Bolus or continuous feeds via a nasogastric tube.
- Bolus or continuous feeds using a pump via a gastrostomy tube.
- Bolus or continuous feeds using a pump via a jejunostomy tube. Intermittent catheterisation and catheter care.
- Care of Mitrofanoff.
- Stoma care, including maintenance of patency of a stoma in an emergency situation using for example the tip of a soft foley catheter where the stoma has been established for less than six months.
- Replacement of gastrostomy button devices in non-urgent and urgent situations once stoma has been well established for more than six months and there have been no problems with the stoma.[16]
- Manual evacuation and enemas as prescribed.

The Royal College of Nursing has also advised that the following tasks should not be undertaken by unregistered and non-health qualified carers:

- Re-insertion of nasogastric tube.
- Re-insertion of percutaneous endoscopic gastrostomy tubes or other gastrostomy tubes (the exception is button devices) and jejunostomy tubes.
- Intramuscular and subcutaneous injections involving assembling syringe or intravenous administration.

---

[15] Routine tracheostomy changes provide an opportunity for a registered practitioner to assess carer competency while also undertaking an assessment of the tracheostomy site.

[16] The first time replacement must be undertaken by an appropriately registered nurse or qualified medical practitioner.

- Programming of syringe drivers.
- Filling of oxygen cylinders (other than liquid oxygen).
- Deep suctioning (oral suctioning tube beyond back of mouth or tracheal suctioning beyond the end of the tracheal tube).[17]
- Siting of indwelling catheters.
- Medicine not prescribed or included in the care plan.
- Ventilation care for an unstable and unpredictable child.

Royal College of Nursing website:
http://www.rcn.org.uk/__data/assets/pdf_file/0013/254200/RCN_Managing_children_with_health_care_needs_delegation_of_clinical_procedures_training_accountability_and_governance_issues_2012_v2.pdf

These lists are provided here as a general guide only and it is important to acknowledge that for children with complex health needs creative and innovative solutions are sometimes required. There will be rare occasions when staff are trained and supported to undertake tasks on the 'non-permitted' list but this will only occur with close supervision and support of a registered health professional.

Training must be carried out by a registered nurse or medical practitioner. It has become common practice for registered nurses working for 'enteral feed companies' to carry out the training of staff. While it is acknowledged that they have expert knowledge about their particular product, they very seldom know the disabled child. It is preferable for support staff to be trained by nurses who know the child as this provides a more child-centred, holistic approach – so feeding is not seen in isolation from other health or impairment issues. The nurse who works with the child should offer ongoing support and monitoring around that procedure.

Similarly, often the technicians working for equipment companies – providing ventilation equipment – are asked to provide training on this equipment. This is appropriate as they know their product, but that training does not replace the need for child-specific training to be provided by a registered nurse or medical practitioner who knows the child.

Once a staff member has been trained, the health professional conducting the training should sign to state that the person is competent to carry out a particular procedure and agree when the training should be updated. The training is not complete until a competency form has been signed. The form used in Wiltshire at the end of specific training is included at the end of this chapter. As described in Chapter 3, in the past there was some reluctance by registered nurses to carry out the training and then sign the competency form as their Code of Practice (2008) held them responsible for the delegation of the tasks.

A way forward was found through the development of competency-based training which clarified for both the health professional and the person being trained what new knowledge they had acquired, what practical tasks they had been trained to do and what they were now being observed as 'competent to do'. In addition, having a clear legal disclaimer that set out the responsibilities of the

---

[17] Deep suction must be undertaken by a registered practitioner as part of a child's chest physiotherapy routine. In exceptional circumstances where there is agreement by the child's medical, nursing and physiotherapy team the task may be delegated by a registered children's physiotherapist as assessed locally where following a risk assessment including vagal stimulation there is no alternative. A written and joint protocol must be agreed locally and risk support mechanisms put in place to support unregistered healthcare support staff and non-health qualified staff in such circumstances.

trainer, the person being trained and the trainee's employer helped health staff overcome their reluctance to carry out the training and organisations' reluctance in allowing their staff to be trained. The wording for the legal disclaimer used in Warwickshire is at the end of this chapter.

The model in relation to clinical procedures developed in the Coventry and Warwickshire area is based on the Steinaker and Bell (1979) model of learning. Training in any clinical procedure involves a theoretical or knowledge based understanding of the procedure and a practical based training for a specific child. The theoretical aspect of each set of competencies has been developed into an e-learning module. Other areas of the country are able to access this training package and both staff and families can then use it. Individuals within that area will be able to register to be trained to a specific level of competency.

The individual will be required to pass an assessment at the end of the theory module before moving on to the individual competency workbooks. A workbook can be created for each child that an individual is being trained to support. Once the individual has successfully completed a workbook, a child-specific sheet and the practical assessment document can be printed off. A registered nurse will then assess the individual and agree when he or she is competent to carry out the task unsupervised. The individual will then be signed off as competent. This training will need to be updated annually.

www.covandwarkschildcomps.org.uk

Experience in children's services with children who require 24 hour or very high levels of support – children on long-term ventilation or with tracheostomies – has shown that it is more cost effective and provides more consistent care if the 'team' supporting the child is built around the child rather than the service. With children who require smaller packages of support, it is common practice for each service to recruit or train their own support staff. However, because of the cost and time it takes to train support staff for children who need very high levels of support, it has become evident that a team of staff should be recruited and trained for a particular child. This means that one member of that team will support the child across all the services they access. For example, from the experience in the Warwickshire and Coventry area, it takes approximately 68 hours to train an individual to support a child with a tracheostomy, 160 hours to train for a child who is ventilator dependent, and 13 hours for gastrostomy training.

The arrangements for the recruitment and employment of support staff varies from one area to another. In some areas the health providers will recruit and employ a team of support staff themselves. These teams of staff will be trained to support one child or a number of children in the area across all environments. In other areas when a child requiring a high level of support is discharged from hospital, health will contract with an outside agency to employ the support staff. It is not within the remit of this book to debate the pros and cons of the different models, but certain elements do need to be considered:

- The size of the support package needs to allow enough time to not only support the child but to train, supervise and support the staff – taking into consideration factors such as travelling time in rural areas.
- More time will be required when initially setting up the support package – as staff become more confident and competent the time will decrease.
- The sustainability of any support package must be considered – particularly when spot purchasing from private agencies. The commissioners do retain responsibility for the service they have commissioned in cases where the support provider is not sustainable.

The issue of vicarious liability is raised where staff support children in different environments. This means that services will have staff they do not employ working in their service. Service managers have corporate responsibility and accountability for the care delivered in their service and, as stated in an earlier section, ultimately legal responsibility rests with the employer who has 'vicarious liability' for their employees. Therefore, in a situation where a child is supported by staff not employed by that particular service, it is essential that the service establishes who will take legal responsibility for the actions of those staff. The advice given in the publication, *A Toolkit to support ventilated children and young people in children's hospices* is as follows:

> *For those services caring for a child/young person in a residential hospice building this may mean that named carers employed by an agency, PCT or local authority will come with them to give care when they are staying at the hospice.*

> *Situations will differ but it is important that children's hospice services establish who will take legal responsibility for the actions of such carers. It is also important to be mindful of the legal and professional accountability of nurses employed within the hospice. In addition children's hospice services should be mindful of the vicarious accountability of the employing hospice: it will retain responsibility for the welfare of the child or young person, even when his or her carers are employed elsewhere.* (Children's Hospices UK 2011, pp.18 – 19)

Following training, support staff need to be offered ongoing support and monitoring by the health professional who carried out the training. This is one of the reasons why it is preferable to use registered nurses employed by the health trust rather than the registered nurse employed by the feed or equipment company or an independent nurse. It means that support is offered within a holistic and child-centred context and the nurse is likely to attend the child's review. Thus the specific clinical procedure is not the focus but rather the whole child.

Moving and handling

Training on moving and handling follows a similar pattern to that required for clinical procedures. Many services, particularly larger ones, may undertake general training for all staff which will give them a good understanding and knowledge of the general principles around 'moving and handling'. The general training needs to be focused on 'children' rather than objects or adults and should be conducted by a trainer approved and experienced in working with children. NHS Trusts have mandatory training processes for clinical staff to ensure the safety of children requiring moving and handling. External services (The Disabled Living Foundation for example) also provide training courses in moving and handling.

Appropriate training ensures that children are always transferred using approved processes. Training in moving and handling needs to be undertaken by all staff carrying out this activity. This training cannot be 'cascaded' by one member of staff attending a course to other members of staff, nor can training around one child be generalised to another child. Although it is good practice to invite parents to attend the training, parents cannot train the support staff. A risk assessment should be carried out on an individual basis for a specific child who requires moving and handling to determine the safest mode of transfer. This plan should be disseminated to all staff involved in supporting this individual.

No one should carry out any moving and handling procedure until they have received accredited training and been deemed competent. Training should always be provided by an accredited trainer. Employers need to offer regular opportunities for staff to update their training. Training should teach safe lifting techniques whilst also highlighting lifts to avoid and the evidence base that has led to the technique being categorised as unsafe. Training needs to ensure that staff are competent and confident to perform their duties safety. The Health and Safety Executive advises that where there are high risk activities such as people handling then regular competency based assessment and monitoring of activities is required and should be documented. Update or refresher training should be provided when competency assessment identifies the need for further training (HSE Briefing Note). Poor skills in a particular technique may be managed by giving advice/demonstration and practice in the workplace or where there are significant issues regarding referral for formal training.

Generally child-specific training is carried out by a physiotherapist, occupational therapist or back care specialist. It is always preferable to use the professional already known to the child. This will mean that the training and any follow-up support will be more holistic and child-centred – rather than moving and handling being seen as an entity separated from the other aspects of the child's life; for instance a child's response to the invasion of their personal space, or the fragility/integrity of their skin.

For children who present a moving and handling risk, staff should be trained in undertaking a risk assessment prior to planning and executing moving and handling. Risk assessment helps to ensure that the safest techniques are identified and then supported through training and or the assistance of equipment. All staff working in an environment where it may be necessary to support a child to move or transfer should have competencies in safe moving and handling practices, ensured by their employer.

Following moving and handling training for a specific child, staff should carry out a risk assessment in order to inform decisions around the safest mode of transfer and then write down the instructions on each move as part of the child's healthcare plan or as a specific moving and handling plan.

Staff will also need training on equipment used for specific children. Equipment, such as hoists and overhead tracking, must be regularly serviced and maintained. There should be an agreement as to who owns the equipment as well as who is responsible for maintaining and servicing it. This applies to equipment used in the child's home by staff and carers who may be employed by the parents through direct payments or individual budgets. It must always be remembered that devices such as wheelchairs should not be used to prevent or control behaviour that challenges. The 'All Wales NHS Manual Handling Training Passport and Information Scheme contains comprehensive advice and best practice information around moving and handling and is applicable to services in England. http://www.wales.nhs.uk/documents/nhs_manual_handling_passpor.pdf

The Scottish Government has, in partnership with Capability Scotland, produced a concise and accessible guide for workers and employers who work with children and young people with moving and handling needs – The Common Sense Approach to Moving and Handling of Disabled Children and Young People. http://www.capability-scotland.org.uk/media/187957/movingandhandlingmobile.pdf

Intimate care

Intimate care can be defined as any care that involves washing, touching or carrying out a procedure to intimate personal areas that most people usually carry out themselves but some children and young people are unable to do because of their young age, physical impairments or other support needs. Examples include care associated with continence and menstrual management as well as tasks such as help with washing or dressing.

All staff who carry out intimate or personal care tasks should receive training, this should include child protection as well as health and safety training in moving and handling. One of the principles in the good practice guidelines (Appendix 1) states that a member of staff should 'never do something unless they know how to do it'. It should therefore not be assumed that because a support staff member carries out intimate tasks with their own children they can carry out intimate care with children they are employed to support.

Training on intimate care should be placed in a wide context rather than purely focus on doing the task. The other issues that should be part of this training are:
- Safeguarding – an understanding of why children who require intimate or personal care are more vulnerable to abuse. Staff should receive training on practices that minimise the risks of abuse.
- An appropriate level of accredited safeguarding training should be ensured prior to employment with children and vulnerable adults.
- All staff working with children and vulnerable adults should receive safeguarding training every three years in line with Working Together guidance (2006).
- Promoting dignity, respect and ensuring privacy – in the way in which intimate care tasks are carried out.
- The importance of promoting a positive image of the child's body.
- An awareness that intimate tasks also need to be carried out in an age appropriate way.

- The need to understand the child's method of communication, particularly where this is predominantly non-verbal so that the support staff can pick up and respond appropriately where the child is indicating pain, discomfort or fear.
- Staff also need to understand the need to discuss the child's needs and preferences and that every effort should be made to ensure that children understand the procedures that are carried out and have some input into how that is done.

Care plans to ensure the above should be documented for children in school, residential, short break or health care settings.

General training

In addition to the training that relates specifically to the three areas covered by this book, services usually offer basic training to all staff in areas such as first aid, child resuscitation and fire safety. Opportunities to refresh and update training should be provided regularly. The organisation or employer should maintain a record of the training staff have received and when that training is due to be updated.

A number of techniques taught on general courses will need to be adapted for children with more complex physical impairments.

References used in this chapter

Children's Hospices UK (2011) *A Toolkit to support ventilated children and young people in children's hospices.* (This organisation is now known as Together for Short Lives.)

HSE Human Factors Briefing Note No. 2: Competence http://www.hse.gov.uk/humanfactors/topics/02competency.pdf

Steinaker, NW and Bell, MR (1979) *The Experiential Taxonomy: A new Approach to Teaching and Learning.* New York: Academic Press.

Resource examples:

Recording Training – Wiltshire Council, Specialist SEN Service.

Legal disclaimer – South Warwickshire NHS Foundation Trust and Coventry and Warwickshire partnership trust.

RECORDING TRAINING
(in a non-school setting)

Record of training given to implement clinical procedure

Brief description of clinical procedure

Nature of training to be given

Name of Trainer

Professional Qualification

Names of carer/s to be trained and role

Dates of training

Has the training been satisfactory?   YES/NO

Date competency was achieved

(Please attach a copy of the competency documentation to this record.)

Signed (Carer) …………………………………………………………………...........………….

Signed (Trainer) …………………………………………………………………...........………..

I agree that the above clinical procedure and training are appropriate to the needs of my patient (name of patient)

Signed (appropriate healthcare professional) ……………….............………………….....

Record of Updates and New Training

Training and Dates	Signature
Clearly state what the training covers	Must be signed by healthcare professional trainer

The following wording is at the end of each competency developed by Coventry and Warwickshire:

I certify that the person named, as carer on this document is competent to carry out the procedure detailed above and that I have current N.M.C. registration.

Overall competency: _____ Date_____

I the above named carer certify that I am happy to carry out the above procedure within the competencies detailed above. I understand the scope of these competencies. I will only use this training in respect of the child specifically named on the front of this form and I will not carry out procedures that are contrary to or not covered by this training.

I will seek further training if I have any concerns about my competency and in any event six weeks before the expiry date on the front of this form renew my training. Upon the date of expiry of this competency, if my training has not been renewed, or if I have concerns about my competency, I will discontinue undertaking the procedure detailed in this document and seek appropriate advice from a suitably qualified clinician and/or my employer. In all other respects I will seek all necessary advice, guidance and further training needed from time to time in order for me to continue to operate within these competencies.

Name: Signature:

Date:

Employers of non NHS trainees.

We will use our best endeavours to ensure that our employee/staff member delivers care to the person named within the boundaries of this competency as outlined above.

Name:

Designation:

Signature: Date:

11. Written information

This brief chapter provides a checklist of the written information that services need to hold in order to safely include children who require clinical procedures, moving and handling and intimate care. The amount and detail of information gathered and stored by a service should be proportionate to the level of service that the child or young person is receiving. This means that schools are likely to hold more information on a child than a youth club attended once a week for three hours.

It is essential that information be gathered from the child, the child's parents, other significant family members and other settings that the child attends to ensure consistency. Using information from other services also helps smaller services that do not have the staff capacity or expertise to collect all the information they may need. It is also critical to optimal transition between pre-school or nursery and school. Information should include:

- An 'All About Me' form or passport with the child or young person's likes or dislikes. Examples are given in Chapters 5 and 6.

- Contact details of family members, other key professionals involved and who to contact in an emergency.

- Information on the child's preferred method of communication – this information may form part of their Communication Passport (see Chapter 6 for more detail). It is also useful for services to have information on where staff can go to obtain additional support or resources if the child uses an alternative form of communication, such as Makaton or a symbol system.

- A care plan – this could be a single plan with specialist plans attached or as modules of that single plan. Specialist plans may include plans on clinical procedures, moving and handling, emergency healthcare, and so on. (Information on plans and examples can be found in Chapter 9.)

- Specialist plans (as listed above) – these can either be part of the main care plan or separate plans. To write some of these plans services may need help from health professionals, such as a children's community nurse to write a plan on administering clinical procedures or a physiotherapist to write a moving and handling plan. Smaller services do need to use and adapt the plans written by larger services.

- Risk assessments that may be specific to children and young people with high support needs, these will also be specific to different settings or activities. (See Chapter 8 for further information on risk assessments and examples of forms.)

- Information on any regular medication that needs to be administered, verified by a medical practitioner. At the end of the chapter is an example of a letter sent out by a short breaks team in Gloucestershire to obtain information from the GP as well as the medication form used by that service.

- If the type of medication or dosage changes, services must be notified in writing. This often causes difficulties for services where children may see the paediatrician during the week and medication is changed with immediate effect. Some services and some doctors have introduced a 'pro-forma' letter that can be signed by the doctor during the clinic appointment and given to services immediately. A copy of the letter used in Nottingham is at the end of this chapter.

- Parental consent to the giving of medication and the carrying out of clinical procedures should be kept by the service. (See Chapter 7 for more information on consent and examples of the forms that can be used.)

Resource examples:

Letter to GP – Gloucestershire County Council, Family Link Service.

Record of Medication – Gloucestershire County Council, Family Link Service.

Letter on change of medication – Nottingham Children's Hospital.

Family Link
Jordans Brook House
North Upton Lane
Barnwood
Gloucester GL4 3TL
Fax: 01452372XXX

Please ask for: JP   **Phone:** 01452 618XXX

Our Ref: JP PG/   **Date:**

Child's Name:

D.O.B:

Address:

Dear GP

I am a Paediatric Nurse working for Family link which is a service that provides short-term breaks for children with disabilities. In order to improve our practice and verify medical information, please can you send/fax a printout medical history for the above named child. I request where possible that this includes:

- The child's diagnosis and/or medical condition
- A record of illnesses and surgical procedures
- All regularly prescribed medication (please complete form enclosed, stating whether the child/young person can manage their own medication safely)
- Medical devices in use
- Immunisation record and any precautions required for safe care practice in the community

A copy of the Medical Authority Form which includes parent's consent to share information is enclosed for your reference.

A pre-paid envelope has been provided for the return of forms enclosed.

Yours sincerely

Miss JP

Family Link Nurse

Prescribed Regular Medication Record

Please use black ink and CLEAR WRITING when filling out this document as policy. Please input CONTROLLED DRUGS onto form (MH1b) as supplied.

Child's Full Name:

Date of Birth:

Any known allergies/sensitivities: Nil known   (Refer to child's care plan)

Generic Medicine Name & Type (tablet, liquid etc)	Strength of Medicine	Dose Prescribed	Route of Administration	Time/s to be Given	Health Professionals Signature/Date

It has/has not been agreed that the child/young person named above is able to safely self administer their own prescribed medicines.

Comments/guidance on self administration (Refer to Care Plan)

Health Professional's Signature..Date.....................

Other signature.. Date.....................

Nottingham Children's Hospital

Nottingham University Hospitals **NHS**
NHS Trust

Children's Centre
City Hospital Campus
Hucknall Road
Nottingham
NG5 1PB
Tel: 0115 8831XXX

URGENT INFORMATION REGARDING MEDICATION

Re: (Child's details)

This patient was reviewed in clinic today and the following medication was started or changed:

Yours sincerely

Signature:

Print Name:

Date:

We are here for you

12. Written records

It is essential that services maintain ongoing records not only to comply with regulations and standards but to ensure that they are continuing to provide a safe service for both children and staff. This chapter provides a checklist of the kinds of written records services need to hold when including children who require clinical procedures, moving and handling and intimate care. Local authorities need to talk to parents who employ personal assistants using direct payments about the written records they will need to maintain.

- Services need to record the routine giving of medication – whether medication has been administered orally or via an enteral tube. An example of the form used by the short break service in Gloucestershire is at the end of this chapter. For children who take a number of medicines at different times of the day, a single 'drug sheet' that stays with the child should be considered. This is particularly important when children are being treated with controlled drugs such as morphine.

- Services should record when medication or another form of rescue treatment is given, for example the administration of Buccal Midazolam or when the magnet is used for children with a VNS (vagus nerve stimulator). In cases when either an adrenaline auto-injector, e.g. EpiPen, is used for a severe allergic reaction or Buccal Midazolam is given and an ambulance is then called, the EpiPen or syringe should be given to ambulance staff. The dose given is then recorded by the ambulance staff and relayed to the staff in the hospital emergency department.

- When an incident occurs where a child or young person potentially or actually injures themselves or others the incident must be recorded.

- Services must keep a record of when staff have received training, who provided the training and when that training is due to be updated.

- If a child uses any equipment, a record should be kept of when it is serviced and maintained. This includes ensuring that equipment in a child's own home is maintained regularly if that is where service provision takes place.

- If a child or young person cannot join in with activities because of their support needs, this should be recorded and discussed at the child's review. These records should contribute in a positive way to future service planning and ensuring that the service becomes more inclusive over time.

- As with all children, if there are child protection concerns more detailed and specific notes or records will need to be kept.

It is important to apply a principle of proportionality to the records that front-line staff are required to keep so that they are not spending an unreasonable amount of time on record keeping and away from direct contact with children and young people.

Where service provision takes place away from the service base, for example in a child's own home or the home of a short break carer, robust systems need to be in place to ensure that the written records of staff and carers are regularly added to the child's main file.

Resource examples:

Recording chart for all medication administered – Gloucestershire County Council, Family Link Service.

MH6a

Recording Chart

for All Medication Administered

Child's Name..

Date of Birth..

Any Known Allergies/Sensitivities...

(Use in conjunction with child/young person's individual care plan)

Note:

Check!! Right child, Right drug, Right dose, Right time and Right Route - **BEFORE** administering **ANY** medication.

189

Child/Young Person's Name .... D.O.B. ....

Generic Medication Name, Type, Strength and Dose to be given as prescribed	Date & Time	Sign	Date & Time	Sign	Date & Time	Sign
VIA	Instructions:					

Generic Medication Name, Type, Strength and Dose to be given as prescribed	Date & Time	Sign	Date & Time	Sign	Date & Time	Sign
VIA	Instructions:					

Generic Medication Name, Type, Strength and Dose to be given as prescribed	Date & Time	Sign	Date & time	Sign	Date & Time	Sign
VIA	Instructions:					

13. Conclusion and checklist

This publication details a process that will assist services, whether specialist or universal, to include disabled children with high support needs. The publication describes 10 areas that need to be considered in order to support children in a safe and inclusive way. The process can be used whether providing direct services or in situations where parents are the employers using direct payments or other forms of personalised budgets.

This checklist will assist the reader to consider whether or not they've considered the issues covered in the chapters; not all will be relevant to every child. The checklist should be used together with the more detailed information in earlier chapters.

Checklist for inclusion

Developing policies and procedures:	Yes	In part	To be developed
Has the drawing up of the policies and procedures involved managers, commissioners, front-line staff (from all agencies) and families? The process should also involve local unions and associations.			
Are they in line with the local area arrangements?			
Does your policy include information on:			
The roles and responsibilities of staff and other carers?			
The roles and responsibilities of all agencies, including funding arrangements for additional support staff?			
The training and support that staff carrying out additional tasks can expect?			
What the service expects from families?			
Insurance or indemnity arrangements?			
Risk management, record keeping?			
Arrangements that will be in place in the case of an emergency?			

Implementing policies	Yes	In part	To be developed
Have all staff read and understood the policies and procedures?			
Is there agreement by all agencies to follow the same policies and procedures?			
Is there a process for monitoring and reviewing policies and procedures?			
Information on the child – working in partnership with the parents	Yes	In part	To be developed
Prior to starting a service with a child who requires a clinical procedure, moving and handling or intimate care, do you have a method of recording information about their disability, support needs and any medical conditions?			
Is your organisation clear about who decides how much and what information will be shared with staff?			
Are there clear principles on which this decision is made?			
Is there a timely process for passing on and receiving information when a child with high support needs moves from one service to another?			
Do staff know where to seek more information about particular conditions or how those conditions may affect a child or young person?			
Are staff clear when they need parental consent?			
Where consent is required from the parent, does the organisation have in place the forms to obtain that consent in writing?			
Partnership with the child or young person	Yes	In part	To be developed
Does your organisation promote the principles of independence and self-reliance of children with high support needs?			
Does your organisation work in a way that ensures all children and young people participate in decisions that affect their lives?			
If the child or young person uses non-verbal communication is the meaning of their non-verbal communication recorded and shared with all staff (for example through the use of a communication passport)?			

	Yes	In part	To be developed
Does your organisation work in a way that ensures the dignity and privacy of children with high support needs is respected at all times?			
Are staff clear about the law on consent as it relates to children and young people?			
Risk assessments and risk management	Yes	In part	To be developed
Have staff received training on risk management?			
Is there clarity on who should conduct the risk assessments?			
Are the risk assessments specific to the child and specific to a procedure?			
Are the risk assessments child-centred, balancing rights and benefits with risks and safeguarding the dignity of the child or young person?			
Does risk management relating to moving and handling consider the use of equipment that is appropriate to the service and encourages as much independence as possible?			
Have families who are employing personal assistants and other support staff been given training and access to their child's risk assessments so that they can put in place the necessary risk assessments expected of employers?			
Plans	Yes	In part	To be developed
Does each child or young person have in place a plan/plans that cover clinical procedures/health needs, moving and handling and intimate care – as appropriate?			
Does each child or young person requiring clinical procedures have a plan that details all of their health needs including the clinical procedures they may require? (This may be part of a larger, more general care plan.)			
Was the plan/s drawn up with the involvement of all staff who hold key information about the child's health needs as well as the parents?			
Does the plan cover:			
The specific procedures that need to be carried out and who should carry them out?			

	Yes	In part	To be developed
Additional risk assessments that may be required and who is responsible for carrying them out?			
Information on how health needs may affect the use of the service – e.g. transport issues?			
Supply, use, storage and maintenance of equipment?			
Individual preferences for how a procedure will be carried out?			
Anticipated changes?			
Arrangements for reviewing the plan?			
Do staff know where the plan/s are kept and can it be accessed by staff who need to read it?			
Are there arrangements in place that mean that the child or young person has a single plan or the plan drawn up by larger services are shared with smaller services as well as families who employ support staff?			
For children and young people who require moving and handling is there an appropriate plan in place? (This may be part of a larger, more general care plan.)			
Is an emergency plan required?			
If so is it in a format that is easy to read and accessible in an emergency?			
Where services are working with groups of children or young people, are strategies in place for summoning assistance in the case of emergencies?			
Training	Yes	In part	To be developed
Clinical procedures – have staff undertaken general training on the most common health conditions, for example epilepsy?			
Is there clarity about who to contact in health when specific training for a procedure is required?			
Is the training on a specific procedure carried out by a registered nurse or medical practitioner who knows the child or young person?			
Is all specific training signed off once the support staff member has been deemed competent to carry it out?			

	Yes	In part	To be developed
Are arrangements for ongoing support by the health 'trainer' in place?			
Are there issues of vicarious liability? If so, has the manager clarified legal responsibility for the actions of staff not employed by the service?			
Moving and handling – is there clarity about who to contact when specific training for an individual child or young person is required?			
Is the training carried out by a trainer who is accredited and competent to work with the child or young person? (Training should preferably be provided by a professional who knows the child.)			
Have staff been given written instructions for carrying out moving and handling tasks?			
Where equipment is used, have staff been trained to use that equipment?			
Intimate care – have staff been trained to carry out intimate care tasks?			
Have staff had safeguarding training that enables them to understand why children with complex healthcare needs may be more vulnerable to abuse?			
Written information	Yes	In part	To be developed
Does the service hold written information about the child or young person that is accessible to the staff working with that child – disability, likes and dislikes, method of communication, emergency contacts etc.?			
Where medication is given, either orally or via an enteral feeding tube, have dosages been verified by a doctor?		n/a	n/a
Is there a process for responding to changes of dosages at short notice?			
Written records	Yes	In part	To be developed
Does the service record the administration of medication and the carrying out of clinical procedures?			
Where the child or young person takes a number of different medicines, has consideration been given to using a single record – agreed by all agencies and the family?			

	Yes	In part	To be developed
Does the service have a protocol on recording and reporting errors in the administration of medication and other procedures?			
Does the service record the specific training received by support staff?			
Is the amount of paperwork completed by staff in proportion to the size of the service received?			
Review and monitoring	Yes	In part	To be developed
Are the clinical procedures, moving and handling and intimate care reviewed at each annual review?			
Are the plans updated as part of the annual review?			
Are the training needs of staff regularly reviewed and updated?			

Acknowledgements

The Council for Disabled Children would like to thank the organisations and services listed below for sharing their examples of good practice, policy documents and forms and giving permission for them to be published in *Dignity and Inclusion*. These examples are provided to stimulate ideas and should assist services when writing policies and drawing up forms. We would recommend that local professionals, practitioners and families should be consulted and that all policies and forms should be appropriate to local circumstances and the nature and size of the service.

Bleasdale School, Lancashire

Birmingham South Central Clinical Commissioning Group

Brighton and Hove City Council and Clinical Commissioning Group

Carers Trust

The Children's Sleep Charity

Cornwall and Isles of Scilly Family Placement Service

Coventry and Warwickshire Partnership Trust and South Warwickshire NHS Foundation Trust

Coventry City Council, Children's Disability Team

Derbyshire County Council, Children and Younger Adults Childcare Improvement Service (Inclusion)

Enfield's Joint Service for Disabled Children

Gloucestershire County Council, Family Link Service

Hackney Learning Trust

Hertfordshire Community NHS Trust

Hertfordshire Strategic Commissioning Group for Children with Complex Care and Additional Needs

Leeds City Council, Family Placement Service

Leeds Teaching Hospitals NHS Trust

Little Breaks, Buckinghamshire

Manchester Metropolitan University

Nottingham University Hospitals NHS Trust in partnership with Nottinghamshire County and NHS Nottingham City, CARIN 4 Families

Nottingham Children's Hospital

Rainbows Hospice for Children and Young People

Sussex Community NHS Trust, Chailey Heritage Clinical Services & Chailey Heritage School

Wiltshire Children and Young People's Community Health Care Planning Working Group

Wiltshire Council Specialist SEN Service

We would also like to thank Steve Broach, Luke Clements and Janet Read for giving us permission to reproduce the extract from *Disabled Children: a legal handbook.*

The Council for Disabled Children would also like to thank the individuals and organisations that gave so willingly of the time and expertise to be on the reference group for this publication:

- Beverley Dawkins, Policy Manager (Profound and multiple learning disabilities), Mencap

- Karen Deacon, Director of Student Operations, Young Epilepsy

- Anne Harris, Director of Care Services, Rainbow Trust Children's Charity

- Antony Julyan, Co-Director, Triangle

- Susan Kelly, National Policy Officer, Short Breaks Network

- Sharon Paley, Development Manager Positive Behaviour Support, British Institute of Learning Disabilities (BILD)

- Linda Partridge, Director of Programmes, WellChild

- Trudy Ward, Head of Children's Community Nursing, Sussex Community NHS Trust

- Ruth Watson, Service Manager, Barnardo's Hamara Family Project

- Dr Mark Whiting, Consultant Nurse, Hertfordshire Community NHS Trust

- David Widdas, Consultant Nurse Children with Complex Health Care Needs, South Warwickshire NHS Foundation Trust and Coventry and Warwickshire Partnership Trust

- Dr Toni Wolff, Paediatrician, Nottingham University Hospitals NHS Trust and British Academy of Childhood Disability representative

And finally, thanks go to the expert readers who gave their comments on the book at final draft stage:

Pamela Shaw, Senior Development Officer, Participation, Council for Disabled Children

Zara Todd, Senior Development Officer, Participation, Council for Disabled Children

Ian Townsend, Advisory Teacher for Physical Impairment, Medway

Philippa Stobbs, Assistant Director, Council for Disabled Children

Dr Anne Gordon, Senior Consultant Occupational Therapist, Evelina London Children's Hospital

Anna Gardiner, Senior Development Officer, Council for Disabled Children